# Sliding with Suzanne

**Judy Upton**

**Methuen**

Methuen

1 3 5 7 9 10 8 6 4 2

Published in Great Britain in 2001 by
Methuen Publishing Limited
215 Vauxhall Bridge Road, London SW1V 1EJ

Copyright © 2001 Judy Upton

The author has asserted her moral rights.

Methuen Publishing Limited Reg. No. 3543167

A CIP catalogue record for this book is available from the British Library

ISBN 0 413 76370 6

Typeset by SX Composing DTP, Rayleigh, Essex
Printed and bound in Great Britain by
Cox & Wyman Ltd, Reading, Berkshire

# Contents

**ROYAL COURT**

out of joint

Out of Joint and Royal Court Theatre present

# SLIDING WITH SUZANNE

by Judy Upton

First performance at the Royal Court Jerwood Theatre Upstairs,
Sloane Square, London on 30 August 2001.

# SLIDING WITH SUZANNE
## TOUR DATES

30 Aug - 22 Sept
**London**
Royal Court Theatre - Box Office: 020 7565 5000

25 - 29 Sept
**Plymouth**
The Drum - Box Office: 01752 267222

2 - 6 Oct
**Liverpool**
Everyman Theatre - Box Office: 0151 709 4776

11 - 13 Oct
**Coventry**
Warwick Arts Centre - Box Office: 02476 524524

15 - 17 Oct
**Brighton**
Gardner Arts Centre - Box Office: 01273 685861

19 & 20 Oct
**Tunbridge Wells**
Trinity Theatre - Box Office: 01892 678678

23 - 27 Oct
**Edinburgh**
Traverse Theatre - Box Office: 0131 228 1404

30 Oct - 3 Nov
**Colchester**
Mercury Theatre - Box Office: 01206 573948

13 - 17 Nov
**Festival De Otono - Madrid**

For information call Out of Joint on 020 7609 0207 or visit
www.outofjoint.co.uk

# SLIDING WITH SUZANNE

by **Judy Upton**

Cast in order of appearance
Josh **Danny Worters**
Luka **Bryan Dick**
Theresa **June Watson**
Suzanne **Monica Dolan**
Ned **Roger Frost**
Sophie **Loo Brealey**


Director **Max Stafford-Clark**
Designer **Julian McGowan**
Lighting Designer **Johanna Town**
Sound Designer **Paul Arditti**
Producer for Out of Joint **Graham Cowley**
Assistant Director **Jacqui Somerville**
Casting Director **Lisa Makin**
Production Manager **Sue Bird**
Company Stage Manager **Cath Binks**
Stage Management **Christabel Anderson, Graham Michael**
Costume Supervisor **Iona Kenrick**
Company Voice Work **Patsy Rodenburg**

Royal Court Theatre would like to thank the following for their help with this production: Wardrobe care by Persil and Comfort courtesy of Lever Fabergé.

# THE COMPANY

**Judy Upton** (writer)
For the Royal Court: Ashes and Sand, Bruises.
Other theatre includes: Everlasting Rose (London
New Play Festival); Temple, The Girlz (Richmond
Orange Tree); The Shorewatchers' House, Stealing
Souls, People on the River (The Red Room);
Sunspots (Red Room/BAC); To Blusher with Love
(The Man in the Moon); Pig in the Middle
(Y Touring); Confidence (Birmingham Rep); The
Ballad of a Thin Man (Channel Theatre Company);
Hotmail from Helsinki (Vienna English Theatre).
Radio includes: Alien Sister (September 2001),
Tissue Memory, Long Time Man (Radio 4).
Screenplays: Ashes and Sand.
Awards include: The Open Stages Competition
1997 for To Blusher with Love, the Verity Bargate
Award 1994 for Bruises and the George Devine
Award 1994 for Ashes and Sand.
Judy Upton is writer-in-residence with the Red
Room Theatre Company.

**Paul Arditti** (sound designer)
Paul Arditti has been designing sound for theatre
since 1983. He currently combines his post as
Head of Sound at the Royal Court (where he has
designed more than 60 productions) with regular
freelance projects.
Royal Court productions include: Clubland, Blasted,
Mouth To Mouth, Spinning Into Butter, I Just
Stopped By To See The Man, Far Away, My Zinc
Bed, 4.48 Psychosis, Fireface, Mr Kolpert, The
Force of Change, Hard Fruit, Other People, Dublin
Carol, The Glory of Living, The Kitchen, Rat in the
Skull, Some Voices, Mojo, The Weir; The Steward
of Christendom, Shopping and Fucking, Blue Heart
(co-productions with Out of Joint); The Chairs
(co-production with Theatre de Complicite);
Cleansed, Via Dolorosa.
Other theatre includes: Tales From Hollywood
(Donmar); Light (Complicite); Our Lady of Sligo
(RNT with Out of Joint); Some Explicit Polaroids
(Out of Joint); Hamlet, The Tempest (RSC);
Orpheus Descending, Cyrano de Bergerac, St Joan
(West End); Marathon (Gate).
Musicals include: Doctor Dolittle, Piaf, The
Threepenny Opera.
Awards include: Drama Desk Award for
Outstanding Sound Design 1992 for Four Baboons
Adoring the Sun (Broadway).

**Loo Brealey**
Theatre includes; Tube! (Union Theatre, Waterloo);
Bloody Poetry (BAC); Can't Stand Up For Falling
Down (Old Red Lion); Final Choice (Watermans
Arts Centre); Rats, The Bear (Piano Store, New
York).
Television includes: The Johnny Vaughan Film Show,
The Blair Witch Phenomenon, Surviving Cannes.
Film includes: Heaven, It was a Bit Like, Pennies
From Heaven (short films).

**Graham Cowley** (producer, Out of Joint)
Out of Joint's Producer since 1998. His long
collaboration with Max Stafford-Clark began
as Joint Stock Theatre Group's first General
Manager for seven years in the 1970s. He
was General Manager of the Royal Court for
eight years, and on its behalf transferred a
string of hit plays to the West End. His career
has spanned the full range of theatre
production, from small fringe companies to
major West End shows and large-scale
commercial tours. Most recently transferred
the Royal Court's production of The Weir to
the West End, produced A Kind of Alaska at
the Edinburgh Festival and in the USA, and
Harry and Me at the Warehouse Theatre,
Croydon.

**Bryan Dick**
Theatre includes: School Play (Soho Theatre).
Television includes: The Bill, Dance with an
Angel, Clocking Off 2, Losing It, North
Square, Shockers II, The Life and Times of
Henry Pratt, Bonjour La Class, Earthfasts,
Speaking in Tongues.
Film includes: Dream.

**Monica Dolan**
For the Royal Court: The Glory of Living.
Other theatre includes: The Walls (RNT);
The Taming of the Shrew, A Midsummer
Night's Dream, Henry V, Coriolanus, Measure
for Measure, Unfinished Business (RSC); Hay
Fever (Savoy/West End); An Experiment with
an Air Pump (Hampstead); The Glass
Menagerie (Royal Lyceum, Edinburgh); Jane
Eyre (Shared Experience tour/Young Vic);
Peter Pan (West Yorkshire Playhouse); Jane
Eyre (York Theatre Royal); To Kill a Mocking
Bird (Northcott Theatre); Outside Edge, The
Merchant of Venice (Exeter).
Television includes: Screen 1: The Gift, The
Bill, Verdict-Rape, Judge John Deed.
Film includes: Topsy Turvy, A Midsummer
Night's Dream.

**Roger Frost**

For the Royal Court: Golgo, Seven Lears, The Last Supper, No End of Blame (and tour), My Night with Reg, Devil's Gateway.

Other theatre includes: Neville's Island (Palace, Watford); Fat Janet is Dead (Warehouse, Croydon); A Jovial Crew, The Winter's Tale, Antony and Cleopatra, Merry Wives of Windsor (RSC); The Seagull (tour, Lilian Bayliss); Ice Cream (Contact, Manchester); The Bacchae (Shared Experience tour); The Miser (Birmingham Rep and tour); Dr Faustus (West End); The Love of a Good Man, Psy Warriors, The Government Inspector, Toad of Toad Hall (Crucible, Sheffield).

Television includes: Bradford In My Dreams, Doc Martin, Midsomer Murders - Destroying Angel, Happy Birthday Shakespeare, Poirot - The Murder of Roger Ackroyd, The Bill, Casualty, Kiss Me Kate, Our Mutual Friend, Prince of Hearts, Out of this World - The Vertical Plane, Accused, Kavangh QC, My Night with Reg, Just William, Milner, Lovejoy, Witchcraft, The Grass Arena, Inspector Morse, A Sense of Guilt, Imaginary Friends, Diary of Adrian Mole, Teddy Bears Picnic, Bergerac, The Monocled Mutineer, Much Ado About Nothing, Pity in History, Eastenders.

Film includes: The Bourne Identity, From Hell, Across the Universe, Christie Malry's Own Double Entry, The Emperor's New Clothes, A Christmas Carol, Room to Rent, Virtual Sexuality, Notting Hill, Shakespeare in Love, What Rats Won't Do, The Village, Young Poisoner's Handbook, Deadly Advice, Time Bandits.

**Julian McGowan** (designer)

For the Royal Court: I Just Stopped By to See the Man, Mr Kolpert, Toast, The Censor, American Bagpipes, The Treatment; The Steward of Christendom, Blue Heart (with Out of Joint).

Other theatre includes: Feelgood (Garrick); Four Nights at Knaresborough (New Vic Workshop at the Tricycle), Enjoy, Blast From the Past, Tess of the D'Urbevilles (West Yorkshire Playhouse); Some Explicit Polaroids (Out of Joint); Waiting for Godot, Don Juan, The Lodger, Women Laughing (Royal Exchange, Manchester); Our Lady of Sligo (Out of Joint/RNT); Our Country's Good (Out of Joint/Young Vic); The Positive Hour (Out of Joint/Hampstead); Shopping and Fucking (Ambassadors/Out of Joint); The Possibilities, Venice Preserv'd, The LA Plays (Almeida); Heart Throb (Bush); The Wives' Excuse (Royal Shakespeare Company); Caesar and Cleopatra, Total Eclipse, A Tale of Two Cities (Greenwich); The Rivals, Man and Superman, Playboy of the Western World, Hedda Gabler.

Opera includes: Cosi Fan Tutte (New Israeli Opera); Eugene Onegin (Scottish Opera); Siren Song (Almeida Opera Festival).

**Jacqui Somerville** (assistant director)

As assistant director, theatre includes: Antigone (Old Vic for Donmar).

As director, theatre includes: Swollen Tongue (Time Out Critics' Choice season, BAC); Toad, Stones of Kolin (New End Theatre); Eclipsed (Teatro Technis); Union Shorts 2, My Sister in this House (Union Theatre); Saving Charlotte (Bridewell); Her Aching Heart (Freedom Theatre and Man in the Moon); Joined at the Head (Man in the Moon); The Tempest (Wakefield Opera House); Tess of the D'Urbevilles (Greenwich Studio Theatre); Joan of Kent (King's Head); Corporal Bluebird (Courageous Petticoats at the Old Bull).

Jacqui was Artistic Director of the Women's Theatre Workshop 1997-98, Associate Director of the Man in the Moon Theatre 1994-96, and runs her own company Courageous Petticoats.

**Max Stafford-Clark** (director)

Founded Joint Stock Theatre Group in 1974 following his Artistic Directorship of The Traverse Theatre, Edinburgh. From 1979 to 1993 he was Artistic Director of the Royal Court. In 1993 he founded Out of Joint. His work as a director has overwhelmingly been with new writing and he has commissioned and directed first productions by many of the country's leading writers.

**Johanna Town** (lighting designer)

Johanna has been Head of Lighting for the Royal Court since 1990 and has designed extensively for the company during this time. Productions include: Spinning into Butter, I Just Stopped By To See The Man, Under the Blue Sky, Mr Kolpert, Other People, Toast, The Kitchen, Faith Healer, Pale Horse, Search and Destroy.

Other recent theatre designs include: Feelgood (Out of Joint/Garrick); Playboy of the Western World (Liverpool Playhouse); Rita, Sue and Bob Too, A State Affair (Out of Joint/Soho Theatre); Arabian Nights (New Victory, New York); Ghosts (Royal Exchange Theatre); Our Lady of Sligo (Irish Repertory Theatre, New York/RNT/Out of Joint); Some Explicit Polaroids, Drummers (Out of Joint); Rose (RNT/Broadway); Little Malcolm (Hampstead/West End); Our Country's Good (Young Vic/Out of Joint); Blue Heart (Royal Court/Out of Joint/New York).

Opera Includes: Tobias and the Angel (Almeida Opera Festival); La Boheme, Die Fledermaus (MTL).

**June Watson**

For the Royal Court: Small Change (also RNT), Saved, Glasshouses, Beside Herself; Blue Heart (Out of Joint), Over Gardens Out, Life Price. Other theatre includes: Il Campiello, State of the Revolution, Sir is Winning, Lark Rise, The Passion, The World Turned Upside Down, The Beggars Opera, As I Lay Dying, Garden of England, Whale, Billy Liar, Machinal, Rutherford & Son, Le Cid, The Prince's Play, Cardiff East, The Long Voyage Home (RNT); Our Lady of Sligo (co-production Out of Joint/RNT); Waiting for the Parade, Middle Age Spread (Lyric); The Ha Ha (Hampstead); Hanky Park (Mermaid); Ballroom (Theatre Royal, Stratford East); Henry IV, V & VI, Richard III, Coriolanus, The Winter's Tale (ESC world tour); Hippolytus (Almeida); Streetcar to Tennessee (Young Vic).

Television includes: Z Cars, Angels, The Further Adventures of Oliver Twist, The Adventures of Caleb Williams, Tales of the Unexpected, Reasons To Be Cheerful, Waterloo Sunset, Skin Deep, The Big H, Eh Brian It's a Whopper, Eastenders, Taggart, The Campbells, Capital City, Snakes & Ladders, The Bill, For the Greater Good, Joe, Inspector Morse, Prime Suspect II, Full Stretch, Taking Over the Asylum, Para Handy, Criminal, Doctor Finlay, A Mug's Game, Common as Muck, Jonathan Creek, Turning World, Wokenwell, Michael and Angelo, Kavanagh QC, Berkeley Square, Where the Heart Is, Holby City, In a Land of Plenty, Thursday the 12th, Brotherly Love, A Great Deliverance.

Film includes: Shoot For the Sun, The Knowledge, Bloody Kids, The Last Yellow, Highlander IV, 102 Dalmations.

**Danny Worters**

Theatre includes: Conversations with My Father (Old Vic); The Cryptogram (Ambassadors); The Life of Galileo (Almeida); The Gingerbread House (Watermans Art Centre); Best Mates (RNT).

Television includes: Casualty, Back Home, Holby City, All the King's Men, The Brokers Man - Series I & II, Children of the New Forest, A Dance to the Music of Time, Bliss, Kiss and Tell, Henry IV Parts I & II, Sorry about Last Night, The All New Alexei Sayle Show, Knowing Me, Knowing You.

Film includes: The Leading Man, Mansfield Park.

## THE ENGLISH STAGE COMPANY
## AT THE ROYAL COURT

The English Stage Company at the Royal Court
opened in 1956 as a subsidised theatre
producing new British plays, international plays
and some classical revivals.

The first artistic director George Devine aimed
to create a writers' theatre, 'a place where the
dramatist is acknowledged as the fundamental
creative force in the theatre and where the play
is more important than the actors, the director,
the designer'. The urgent need was to find a
contemporary style in which the play, the acting,
direction and design are all combined. He
believed that 'the battle will be a long one to
continue to create the right conditions for
writers to work in'.

Devine aimed to discover 'hard-hitting,
uncompromising writers whose plays are
stimulating, provocative and exciting'. The Royal
Court production of John Osborne's Look Back
in Anger in May 1956 is now seen as the decisive
starting point of modern British drama and the
policy created a new generation of British
playwrights. The first wave included John
Osborne, Arnold Wesker, John Arden, Ann
Jellicoe, N F Simpson and Edward Bond. Early
seasons included new international plays by
Bertolt Brecht, Eugène Ionesco, Samuel Beckett,
Jean-Paul Sartre and Marguerite Duras.

The theatre started with the 400-seat
proscenium arch Theatre Downstairs, and then
in 1969 opened a second theatre, the 60-seat
studio Theatre Upstairs. Some productions
transfer to the West End, such as Caryl
Churchill's Far Away, Conor McPherson's The
Weir, Kevin Elyot's Mouth to Mouth and My
Night With Reg. The Royal Court also co-pro-
duces plays which have transferred to the West
End or toured internationally, such as Sebastian
Barry's The Steward of Christendom and Mark
Ravenhill's Shopping and Fucking (with Out of
Joint), Martin McDonagh's The Beauty Queen Of
Leenane (with Druid Theatre Company), Ayub
Khan-Din's East is East (with Tamasha Theatre
Company, and now a feature film).

Since 1994 the Royal Court's artistic policy has
again been vigorously directed to finding and
producing a new generation of playwrights. The
writers include Joe Penhall, Rebecca Prichard,
Michael Wynne, Nick Grosso, Judy Upton,
Meredith Oakes, Sarah Kane, Anthony Neilson,
Judith Johnson, James Stock, Jez Butterworth,
Marina Carr, Simon Block, Martin McDonagh,
Mark Ravenhill, Ayub Khan-Din, Tamantha
Hammerschlag, Jess Walters, Che Walker, Conor
McPherson, Simon Stephens, Richard Bean, Roy
Williams, Gary Mitchell, Mick Mahoney, Rebecca

photo: Andy Chopping

Gilman, Christopher Shinn, Kia Corthron, David
Gieselmann, Marius von Mayenburg and David
Eldridge. This expanded programme of new
plays has been made possible through the
support of A.S.K Theater Projects, the Jerwood
Charitable Foundation, the American Friends of
the Royal Court Theatre and many in association
with the Royal National Theatre Studio.

In recent years there have been record-
breaking productions at the box office, with
capacity houses for Jez Butterworth's Mojo,
Sebastian Barry's The Steward of Christendom,
Martin McDonagh's The Beauty Queen of
Leenane, Ayub Khan-Din's East is East, Eugène
Ionesco's The Chairs, David Hare's My Zinc Bed
and Conor McPherson's The Weir, which
transferred to the West End in October 1998
and ran for nearly two years at the Duke of
York's Theatre.

The newly refurbished theatre in Sloane Square
opened in February 2000, with a policy still
inspired by the first artistic director George
Devine. The Royal Court is an international
theatre for new plays and new playwrights, and
the work shapes contemporary drama in Britain
and overseas.

**out of joint**

Founded in 1993, Out of Joint is a national and international touring theatre company dedicated to the production of new writing. Under the direction of Max Stafford-Clark the company has premiered plays from leading writers including Sebastian Barry, Caryl Churchill, Mark Ravenhill and Timberlake Wertenbaker, as well as first-time writers such as Simon Bennett.

*"Britain's most successful touring company"*
**The Stage**

Touring all over the UK, Out of Joint frequently performs at and co-produces with key venues including Hampstead Theatre, the Liverpool Everyman & Playhouse, the Royal Court, the Royal National Theatre, Soho Theatre and the Young Vic. By co-producing its work the company is able to maintain a large on-going repertoire as well as premiering at least two new plays a year. Out of Joint is classed as one of the British Council's 'flagship' touring companies, with regular international tours to countries including India, Bulgaria, Russia, Egypt, Brazil, Australia, New Zealand, USA and many parts of Europe. Back home, Out of Joint also pursues an extensive education programme, with workshops in schools, universities and colleges as well as producing resource packs designed for each production.

*"Max Stafford-Clark's brilliant company"*
**The Scotsman**

Out of Joint's challenging and high-profile work has gained the company an international reputation and awards including the prestigious Prudential Award for Theatre. With a permanent commitment from the Arts Council of England, Out of Joint continues to commission, develop and produce new writing of the highest calibre.

*"the excellent Out of Joint"*
**Daily Telegraph**

| Director | **Max Stafford-Clark** |
| Producer | **Graham Cowley** |
| Marketing Manager | **Alice Lascelles** |
| Administration & Education Manager | **Laura Collier** |
| PA to Artistic Director & Assistant Director | **Jacqui Somerville** |
| Literary Adviser | **Lee White** |
| Finance Officer | **Sharon Smith** |

Board of Directors: Kate Ashfield, Linda Bassett, John Blackmore (Chair), Elyse Dodgson, Sonia Friedman, Stephen Jeffreys, Paul Jesson, Karl Sydow

**Are you on the OJO mailing list?**
For information on upcoming shows, tour details and offers, send us your contact details, letting us know whether you'd like to receive information by post or email.

**OJO education work**
Out of Joint offers a diverse programme of workshops and discussions for groups coming to see Sliding with Suzanne. If you would like to know more about our Autumn Education Programme, the Resource Packs or Our Country's Good workshops then contact Max or Laura at Out of Joint.

**OJO contact details**
Please note our new postal address from Sept '01. All other details stay the same.

| Post: | Out of Joint, 7 Thane Villas, Thane Works, London N7 7PH |
| Tel: | 020 7609 0207 |
| Fax | 020 7609 0203 |
| Email | ojo@outofjoint.co.uk |

Out of Joint is grateful to the following for their support over the years:
The Arts Council of England, The Foundation for Sport and the Arts, The Baring Foundation, The Paul Hamlyn Foundation, The Olivier Foundation, The Peggy Ramsay Foundation, The John S Cohen Foundation, The David Cohen Charitable Trust, The National Lottery through the Arts Council of England, The Prudential Awards, Stephen Evans, Karl Sydow, Harold Stokes and Friends of Theatre, John Lewis Partnership, Royal Victoria Hall Foundation

THE ARTS COUNCIL OF ENGLAND

Emma Rydal and Emily Aston in the double bill Rita, Sue and Bob Too/A State Affair. (Photo: John Haynes)

## Future OJO projects

Following a hugely successful 2000/01 tour, Out of Joint are pleased to be reviving their double bill Rita, Sue and Bob Too/A State Affair for Winter 2001. As well as returning to London's Soho Theatre in December, the production will be going to the West Yorkshire Playhouse and embarking on an international tour to countries including Australia, New Zealand and the USA.

In the new year, Out of Joint will be premiering Hinterland, the eagerly-awaited new play from Sebastian Barry, author of Steward of Christendom and Our Lady of Sligo. This co-production with the Abbey Theatre Dublin and the Royal National Theatre will begin a national tour at the Bolton Octagon, followed by visits to the Abbey, the National's Cottesloe Theatre as well as several further dates still to be announced.

For more information on upcoming OJO shows, either join the mailing list (see the opposite page for details) or visit www.outofjoint.co.uk

## OJO shows to date

| | |
|---|---|
| **2001** | Sliding with Suzanne by Judy Upton<br>Feelgood by Alistair Beaton |
| **2000** | Rita, Sue and Bob Too by Andrea Dunbar & A State Affair by Robin Soans |
| **1999** | Some Explicit Polaroids by Mark Ravenhill<br>Drummers by Simon Bennett |
| **1998** | Our Country's Good by Timberlake Wertenbaker<br>Our Lady of Sligo by Sebastian Barry |
| **1997** | Blue Heart by Caryl Churchill<br>The Positive Hour by April De Angelis |
| **1996** | Shopping & Fucking by Mark Ravenhill |
| **1995** | The Steward of Christendom by Sebastian Barry<br>Three Sisters by Anton Chekhov & The Break of Day by Timberlake Wertenbaker |
| **1994** | The Man of Mode by George Etherege & The Libertine by Stephen Jeffreys<br>The Queen and I by Sue Townsend & Road by Jim Cartwright |

## REBUILDING THE ROYAL COURT

In 1995, the Royal Court was awarded a National Lottery grant through the Arts Council of England, to pay for three quarters of a £26m project to completely rebuild its 100-year old home. The rules of the award required the Royal Court to raise £7.6m in partnership funding. The building has been completed thanks to the generous support of those listed below.

We are particularly grateful for the contributions of over 5,700 audience members.

English Stage Company Registered Charity number 231242.

## THE AMERICAN FRIENDS OF THE ROYAL COURT THEATRE

AFRCT support the mission of the Royal Court and are primarily focused on raising funds to enable the theatre to produce new work by emerging American writers. Since this not-for-profit organisation was founded in 1997, AFRCT has contributed to seven productions including Rebecca Gilman's Spinning Into Butter. They have also supported the participation of young artists in the Royal Court's acclaimed International Residency.

If you would like to support the ongoing work of the Royal Court, please contact the Development Department on 020 7565 5050.

THE ARTS COUNCIL OF ENGLAND

## PROGRAMME SUPPORTERS

The Royal Court (English Stage Company Ltd) receives its principal funding from London Arts. It is also supported financially by a wide range of private companies and public bodies and earns the remainder of its income from the box office and its own trading activities.

The Royal Borough of Kensington & Chelsea gives an annual grant to the Royal Court Young Writers' Programme and the London Boroughs Grants Committee provides project funding for a number of play development initiatives.

The Jerwood Charitable Foundation continues to support new plays by new playwrights through the Jerwood New Playwrights series. Since 1993 the A.S.K. Theater Projects of Los Angeles has funded a Playwrights' Programme at the theatre. Bloomberg Mondays, the Royal Court's reduced price ticket scheme, is supported by Bloomberg.

LONDON ARTS

# FOR THE ROYAL COURT

# Sliding with Suzanne

*For my family*

# Act One

## Scene One

*A Seven–Eleven type convenience shop. Brighton. Night. Seventeen-year-old* **Josh** *is on the till, reading* FHM. *Outside the window, sixteen-year-old* **Luka** *is gingerly prodding a hedgehog in the kerb with the toe of his trainer. He hesitates, crouches down to look at it, stands again and suddenly stamps on it hard, repeatedly.* **Josh** *looks up from his magazine, sees* **Luka** *stomping on the hedgehog, is disgusted.* **Luka** *peels the hedgehog off the kerb, picks it up and enters the shop, he takes a can of Red Bull from the fridge, comes up to the counter.*

**Josh** *is staring at the hedgehog pancake.* **Luka***'s hand is bloody.*

**Josh**   Er . . . have you got proof of age? I have to ask everyone.

**Luka** *walks behind the counter takes a bottle of vodka from the shelf, puts it down beside the Red Bull. He takes out a couple of crumpled notes to pay, dumps them on the counter.* **Josh** *puts the bar-code reader on the Red Bull, then picks up the vodka bottle, hesitates, weighing up whether to risk a confrontation.* **Luka** *is examining the hedgehog.*

**Josh**   I can't let you have this, I'm afraid.

**Luka**   Why not?

**Luka** *puts the hedgehog down on the counter.*

**Josh**   That's sick. That's murder. I'm calling the RSPCA. (**Luka** *hesitates, then punches* **Josh** *hard in the face.*) Shit.

**Luka** *takes the bottle and Red Bull and leaves.* **Josh** *holds his nose.*

**Luka** *exits.* **Josh** *has a nosebleed, his eyes are watering.* **Josh** *exits, among the shelves.*

**Theresa** *enters. She is around sixty. With her is her thirty-five-year-old daughter* **Suzanne**. *They approach the shop.* **Josh** *enters, dabbing at his nose with some bog roll.*

**Josh** (*to himself*)   Shit.

**Theresa**    Grab a basket.

**Suzanne** *walks ahead.*

**Josh**    Excuse me.

**Theresa**    Pick up a basket.

**Suzanne** *ignores her.* **Theresa** *picks up a basket, starts shopping.*

**Josh**    Excuse me, we're closing in a minute.

**Theresa**    Thank you, we won't be long.

**Josh** *shrugs. From behind the counter,* **Josh** *takes a long-handled floor brush. He uses it to knock the hedgehog on the floor.* **Suzanne** *notices, watches, puzzled. He pushes the hedgehog along the floor, then taking a swing at it with the brush, sends it flying out the door, and turns the sign on the door to 'closed'.)*

**Theresa**    I wish you'd let me know you were coming. If you'd just thought to ring, Suzanne. I'd have gone up Safeway's. They're so much cheaper than here.

**Suzanne**    Yeah, okay, hurry up, Mum.

**Theresa**    I don't see anything of you for months at a time and then you just turn up. Out of the blue.

**Suzanne**    You don't want to see me? You don't want to see me, is that it?

**Theresa**    It only takes a minute to phone. I can't just be expected to drop everything for you, can I? I might have had my own plans for the evening, but oh no, that wouldn't enter your little head, would it?

**Josh** *goes back behind his counter, takes a spray bottle of disinfectant, sprays and scrubs his counter.*

**Suzanne**    Your own plans? Like you've started going to bingo or something?

*Pause.* **Theresa** *picks up a box of orange juice.*

**Theresa**    One pound seventy – for juice?

*She puts it back.*

**Suzanne**    Look, there wasn't time, I told you.

**Theresa**    You could've phoned me from the station.

**Suzanne**    There wasn't time, Mum!

**Theresa**    Wasn't time to pick up the phone. Wasn't time to make one little call?

**Suzanne** (*mutters*)    Oh fuck off.

**Theresa**    Yes, that's right. Use that language. That's all there is with you.

**Theresa** *continues to shop.*

**Suzanne**    What's that supposed to mean?

**Theresa**    Beans or pasta shapes?

**Suzanne**    What do you mean by 'that's all there is with you'? You always say that, and it doesn't mean shit. 'That's all there is with you.' You just open your mouth and spout rubbish.

**Theresa**    I'm not the only one.

**Suzanne**    Fuck off.

**Theresa**    That's what I mean – swearing, being unpleasant, all of the time. I mean that's probably why it happened, isn't it? You started treating him like you treat me.

**Suzanne**    Shit – I told you what happened. I fucking sat down and explained the whole thing to you.

**Theresa**    You said he told you he didn't want to live with you any more.

**Suzanne**    It wasn't his decision. You don't know what they do – how they operate. They poisoned him against me.

**Theresa**    But earlier you said –

**Suzanne**   Just listen to me right! For once in your life, okay? They poisoned him. Joanna pretending to be my friend, and saying 'I'm there for you', the two-faced bitch. Saying the cooker's dangerous, saying we need Rentokil back for the mice. Always having her little talks with him, snooping into our life. 'Suzanne went where? Who was she with?' I don't know what he's told her . . . I mean he doesn't know what's going on in his own head half the time, crazy thoughts . . . Joanne says he's 'got some issues' and then won't fucking explain. You gotta help me, Mum. I wouldn't have wasted the fucking train fare coming down here – £13.65 – fuck! – if I'd have thought all you'd worry about was what to have for fucking dinner. And you don't have a clue, do you?

**Theresa**   A clue about –

**Suzanne**   About what I should do! What should I do, Mum? Tell me what I should do to get him back?

**Theresa**   Well, I . . .

**Suzanne**   I mean, what's the time now anyway?

**Theresa**   Elevenish.

**Suzanne**   I'm not hungry, and it's too late for dinner now.

**Theresa**   It won't take long to prepare.

**Suzanne**   I've no appetite. That train smelt like shit, like the toilet had overflowed or something. And all the windows were stuck . . . well, one of them wasn't, but every time I opened it, this bloke shut it again. I nearly fucking decked him, I told him there are people suffocating in here, and if you like the smell of shit so much, Mr-Fucking-Awkward-Bastard, then why don't you stick your head up your arse?

**Theresa**   I've a tin of leek soup, which I know you like . . .

**Suzanne**   I don't. I've never liked it. Leek soup? I've never ate it, and never fucking will as long as I live . . .

**Theresa**   Well, you can suit yourself then, can't you?

**Suzanne**   I'm gonna page him. (*She goes up to the till.*) You got a phone here?

**Josh**   No, sorry.

**Suzanne** (*sees the phone behind him*)    See that? See there? What's that? That looks like a phone to me.

**Josh**   Yeah, but you can't –

**Suzanne** *goes behind the counter, pushing him aside. She picks up the phone, dials.* **Josh** *wipes his nose, it's still bleeding a bit.*

**Theresa**   You still vegetarian?

**Suzanne**   What? Yeah. (*On phone.*) Hallo?

**Theresa**   You'll eat a little fish?

**Suzanne**   No, I won't eat a little fucking fish, Mum! (*On phone.*) Hallo? Sorry. Yeah, a message to 07699 68752. Yeah. It's . . . 'Call me. Urgent.' Alright, 'urgently' – what are you, some fucking grammar expert? 'Call me. Urgently.' That's it, yeah. He'll know. Okay, okay, put 'love Suzanne' and some kisses. You know, 'X's. About three. No, put four. Four kisses yeah. Wait a minute, can you just check for me . . . I sent him another message about an hour ago . . .

**Theresa**   Though you didn't have time to call me?

**Suzanne**   Shut up! I can't hear. (*On phone.*) You sent it? You're sure? Okay. Okay. Ta. (*She puts the phone down. To* **Josh**.) Thanks.

**Josh** (*insincerely*)    No problem.

**Suzanne** (*to* **Theresa**)    We've got matching pagers. His 'n' hers.

**Suzanne** *flashes her pager.*

**Theresa**   I don't understand those things.

**Suzanne** *goes back to the phone, slipping behind* **Josh** *before he notices her. She starts dialling another number.*

**Josh**  Hey, why don't you go outside and use the phone box?

**Suzanne**  Keep your hair on. I'll pay. I'll pay in a minute.

**Josh**  You can't pay, it's not a payphone.

**Suzanne**  See my arse? Kiss it.

**Suzanne** *listens for a moment, then slams the phone down.*

**Theresa**  Suzanne . . . love . . .

**Suzanne**  Pasta shapes.

**Theresa**  What?

**Suzanne**  Don't just stand there dithering in front of the fucking shelf. I've told you what I want. The pasta shapes. (**Theresa** *goes to pick a large can.*) Just a small one. I'm not gonna be here tomorrow.

**Theresa** (*looks at her basket of shopping*)  But I've just stocked up for the whole week!

**Suzanne**  A week? What makes you think I'd spend a week with you? Half-hour I've been back. Half-hour and you're getting on my tits.

**Theresa** *puts the basket down. She wipes her eyes.*

**Theresa**  That's all there is with you!

**Suzanne**  What! Fuck! I can't believe you said that again. I can't believe it, Mum. God, you just do it on purpose, don't you? 'That's all there is with you' – what does it mean? Why do you always say that!

**Theresa**  I've had enough. I don't hear a word, not a word for three months, you don't phone, you don't answer the phone . . .

**Suzanne**  Mum, listen to me –

**Theresa**  You don't worry about me, do you? Don't give me a thought. I might as well be dead –

**Suzanne** Oh don't fucking start that –

**Theresa** I could be lying dead on the floor, and you wouldn't know.

**Suzanne** Okay, okay, I'll phone you more. I'll phone you every day. And if you're lying dead on the fucking floor, a lot of good that's gonna do. It's really gonna help, that – me phoning.

**Theresa** Oh it's alright for you –

**Suzanne** It's not alright for me! How can you fucking say that! You never listen, do you, you stupid old bat!

**Theresa** I'm not being sworn at –

**Suzanne** I did not –

**Theresa** I'm not being shouted at. You get what you want to eat, and you pay for it. I'm going home.

**Suzanne** Mum. Mum?

**Theresa** *exits, leaving the shopping basket.* **Suzanne** *notices* **Josh** *is smiling, more out of nervousness than anything. She starts to walk over to him. He stops smiling.*

**Suzanne** You waiting to close up?

**Josh** Er . . . when you're ready.

*She puts the shopping basket on the counter.*

**Suzanne** Just ring up five quid's worth. That's all I've got on me.

**Josh** Up to five quid?

**Suzanne** I've got five quid, forty-three. Last of the big spenders. No . . . wait, give me four quid's worth. Gotta leave enough for my bus fare, and most of it'll only get sicked up anyway.

**Josh** *starts ringing up the shopping.* **Suzanne** *looks at her pager. Still no message.*

**Josh**   Do you want the apples?

**Suzanne**   What?

**Josh**   I mean, they're a bit pricey and they don't go with anything else, do they, apples?

**Suzanne**   You don't eat apples? What're your teeth like?

**Josh**   Fine.

**Suzanne**   Yeah? Show me?

**Josh** *continues to ring up the shopping. She tries to look at him.*

**Suzanne**   What happened to your nose?

**Josh** (*rubs his nose*)   It looks really bad?

**Suzanne**   Like a truck hit it.

**Josh**   Thanks. (**Suzanne** *bites into an apple.*) Do you want the apples rung up?

**Suzanne**   No, I'm all done with them.

**Josh**   Three pounds, seventy-two then.

**Suzanne**   Can you put in it two bags – one inside the other. (**Josh** *is about to.*) No, let me do it, you're getting blood everywhere. (**Suzanne** *puts her groceries in a bag. She pays, looks at her change.*) Not really got enough left for a drink, have I? Without breaking into the bus fare.

**Josh**   Wanna look in the fridge?

**Suzanne**   I mean a sit-down-in-the-pub kind of drink.

**Josh**   It's cheaper to buy it here than at rip-off pub prices.

**Suzanne**   Yeah, but I want to sit down. (*Pause.*) Can I sit down here?

**Josh**   I'm closing up.

*She opens a beer can, one of a four-pack.*

**Josh**   Hey!

**Suzanne** (*perches on the edge of the counter.* **Josh** *starts to cash up.* *She spreads her change on the counter*)    I'd buy you one and all if I had enough. Don't like drinking alone. I get all morbid. (*She counts the money.*) Couldn't lend me 39p, could you?

**Josh**    No.

**Suzanne**    I'm a pain in the arse I know. (**Josh** *takes 39p from his pocket, puts it with* **Suzanne**'*s money and rings it up.*) You're a treasure.

**Josh**    I've gotta make the till balance.

**Suzanne**    I'll borrow it off my mum and bring it in, in the morning.

**Josh** (*preoccupied, locking the till*)    Yeah right.

**Suzanne** (**Josh** *turns to look at the beers in the fridge*)    Getting tempted?

**Josh**    Yeah, you've made me want one myself now.

**Suzanne**    I won't tell. (*He takes a beer from the fridge.*) You don't have to pay?

**Josh**    Dream on. I'll put the money in tomorrow.

*He opens his beer. Then goes and dims the lights.*

**Suzanne**    Very atmospheric.

**Josh**    Just in case my boss walks by.

**Suzanne**    Ah. (*She walks up to* **Josh** *and clinks her can against his.*) Cheers. (*They drink in silence.*) Are you old enough to be drinking?

**Josh**    Yeah.

**Suzanne**    God's honest? (*Pause.*) You need to clean that up. (*She wipes a little blood off his face with her finger.*)

**Josh**    Don't know if it's mine or the hedgehog's.

**Suzanne**    Hedgehog?

**Josh**    Don't ask. Not got a mirror, have you?

**Suzanne**    No. I stopped carrying a bag. I lost so many. (*She takes a tissue from her pocket.*) Don't worry, it's clean. (*She wipes his face.*) That looks a bit better. Get your mum to have a look when you get home.

**Josh** (*sips his beer*)    Don't live with my mum.

**Suzanne**    So what happened?

**Josh**    With my mum?

**Suzanne**    What? With your nose. Someone hit you?

**Josh**    A customer, yeah. A schizoid customer.

**Suzanne** *reaches over and ruffles his hair. He looks at her surprised.* **Suzanne** *takes out her purse.*

**Suzanne**    Let's have another beer.


**Scene Two**

**Theresa**'s *kitchen. Night.*

**Theresa** *and* **Ned** (*aged fifty-five*) *are sipping wine. They are both slightly tense and awkward.*

**Theresa**    Seems like our special dinner wasn't meant to be . . .

**Ned**    I saw your light was still on. And your note said there'd been a bit of a crisis . . . I was worried.

**Theresa**    I'm sorry Ned, I didn't know what to put really. I know I can't ring you when you're driving . . .

**Ned**    And I hadn't counted on getting delayed. Only one carriageway and speed restrictions on the A27. If only I'd taken the 2032.

**Theresa**    You must be tired. It's really been one of those days. I was so surprised when Suzanne just turned up. I suppose it's lucky I hadn't started cooking. I was gonna make something special . . . a chicken risotto. But Suzanne's a vegetarian you see. Otherwise it could've done all of us. At least have another glass of wine.

**Ned**    Not for me, thanks

*Pause.*

Maybe we were pushing things on . . . you know, faster than they were meant to go.

**Theresa**    Do you feel that?

**Ned**    Well, I wouldn't want it to spoil our friendship in any way . . .

**Theresa**    Yes, I understand. Maybe it would change things too much.

*Pause.*

**Ned**    I should be making a move.

*He stands up.*

**Theresa**    Oh. Oh right.

*She takes the glasses to the sink, and moves as if to show him out.*

**Theresa**    Typical Suzanne, ruining everything. And I don't even know where she is . . . We had words, up the shop. She should've been back by now.

**Ned**    She won't be long, I'm sure.

**Theresa** *sits down.*

**Theresa**    Well, you see she's got the groceries so I can't make her anything until she gets here. Not that I really want to eat now it's got so late, and I think she probably still has problems with food. I can never really get to the bottom of it. She loved fish fingers when she was a kid. Used to get ketchup all over her face.

**Ned**    She seemed to be eating okay when she brought that little Zoe down.

**Theresa**    Yes, that's right. Zoe wouldn't do anything unless Suzanne did it first . . . well she had to eat then, and eat properly too.

*Pause.*

But she seems to be having some worries with that boy.

**Ned**    Is he the same one she brought down at Christmas?

**Theresa**    Yeah. Been with her nearly six months now.

**Ned**    A really nice lad, and that puppy . . .

**Theresa**    Sweet little thing – but into everything. Chewed up my chiffon scarf . . . Oh and flattened your roses.

**Ned**    They survived.

**Theresa**    Ned . . . I was in that little antique shop earlier, the one at Preston Circus. I do sometimes . . . just pop in, to have a bit of a look. Anyway I noticed they'd got a box with a couple of maps in, old ones they looked like. One was of Exeter, I remember that, the other, some place in Scotland.

**Ned**    Were they Ordinance Survey?

**Theresa**    Yeah, I think so. They'd both got paintings on the cover – like some of yours have. One of 'em was really pretty – a car, I think . . . though I couldn't make out all the detail. Well, you know my eyes.

**Ned**    What colour were the covers?

**Theresa**    I . . . I'm not sure I remember.

**Ned**    I've got all the editions for Exeter, but the Scottish one . . . I suppose you can't remember where . . .

**Theresa**    No, I . . . it began with a 'D', I think . . . Not a place I've heard of.

**Ned**    Dundee?

**Theresa**    I've heard of Dundee.

**Ned**    There're a few Scottish ones I still need.

**Theresa**    I should've written it down . . .

**Ned**    No, no, it's no problem, I can pop in myself in the morning. I'm not working tomorrow . . . Just in case. Sometimes they tend to go pretty quick.

**Theresa**    You'll curse me if it's gone, won't you?

**Ned**    Of course not, Theresa.

*Pause.*

Friday week, Michael and his wife are coming down.

**Theresa**    That's nice.

**Ned**    I thought maybe you might like to come to dinner.

**Theresa**    If I wouldn't be –

**Ned**    You wouldn't.

*She walks up to him.*

**Theresa**    I'm glad you came round, Ned.

*She touches his face. There's a possibility of a kiss but while they are hesitating, the doorbell rings.*

**Theresa**    Took her time, didn't she?

*Exit* **Theresa**.

**Theresa** (*off*)    Luka! Where did you spring from?

*Enter* **Theresa** *with* **Luka**.

**Luka**    Alright, Mr Bisset?

**Theresa**    Suzanne's been worrying herself sick.

**Luka**    Where is she?

**Theresa**    Out of her mind with stress and anxiety, that's what she is.

**Luka** (*calls out*)   Suzanne!

**Theresa**   She's not here. She's up the shop.

**Luka**   Yeah, like she didn't bother to let me know she was heading down here. I had to go crawling 'round all her stupid friends, and ex-boyfriends, then I see Vicky, the gobby cow who says 'Uh, she's gone to her mum's.' (*Sarky.*) Nice of her to tell me, you know.

**Theresa**   She came to ask me what to do.

**Luka**   Do about what? Me? It ain't me with the problem, I can tell you . . .

*He sits down at the table.*

**Theresa**   They're like that, all my kids, any trouble they come running back to their mum.

**Luka**   Is she in trouble?

**Theresa**   No, dear, I just meant –

**Luka**   I had to hide in the train loo all the way down here, cos I couldn't pay the fare. I haven't got any money cos she's already borrowed my allowance this week.

**Ned** (*gets up*)   I really should be making a move, Theresa.

**Theresa**   Oh . . . oh alright. (*She goes to him, wants to kiss him goodbye but doesn't find an opportunity*.) See you on Friday . . . if not before.

**Ned**   Friday? Oh yes.

**Theresa**   Goodnight.

**Ned** *exits*. **Luka** *starts unlacing his trainers.*

**Theresa**   Are those muddy?

**Luka**   Bloody. I had to kill a hedgehog.

**Theresa**   What? You had to –

**Luka**    A car had hit it. Its guts were out but it was still moving.

**Theresa**    Oh God, Luka.

**Luka**    Do you ever worry about stuff like that? Or dream about it?

**Theresa**    What dear? Dead hedgehogs?

**Luka**    Disembowelment.

*Pause.*

**Theresa**    No. No, dear, I can't say I do. (*Pause.*) Luka, if you don't mind me asking . . . what happened between you and my daughter? I mean, did you have a bit of a disagreement?

**Luka**    You could say that.

**Theresa**    But that's still no excuse for running off, worrying everyone –

**Luka**    I hadn't run off.

**Theresa**    Suzanne thought you'd run away. Or gone to social services.

**Luka**    I just needed a bit of space, okay.

**Theresa**    You can't just go off when it suits you. That's really thoughtless, Luka.

**Luka**    It wasn't thoughtless . . . I'd been thinking about it for days, weeks really.

**Theresa**    You're not happy at my daughter's? She is argumentative, I'll give you that . . .

**Luka**    I'd reached my limit.

**Theresa**    Can you tell me what it was about?

**Luka**    Coming in late.

**Theresa**    You stayed out till when?

**Luka**   She stayed out. Till four a.m. Drinking.

**Theresa**   Well, I . . .

**Luka**   She wouldn't say where she'd been. I said some stupid stuff – and she start yelling cos she was pissed and that. So I started breaking things – mugs and a plate. Just to make her listen. (**Theresa** *stands up.*) It was stupid. Sometimes I just get so jealous, I don't know.

**Theresa**   Jealous of what?

**Luka**   Jealous she can do anything she wants.

**Luka** *checks his pager.*

**Theresa**   You've got a pager too. Oh of course, Suzanne was trying to get you on it earlier. What does it do? (*He shows her, she squints to read the messages.*) They're amazing, these modern things.

**Luka**   Modern – I wish. It's so out of date, I can't let people at school see it. Have to pretend I've a mobile with text messaging.

**Theresa**   Shop must've closed by now. Maybe she's popped in to see one of her old friends.

**Luka**   Girls, or . . . ?

**Theresa**   Girls she was at school with, yes. Women they are now, of course. Maria's in the post office and Michelle's a ward sister at the Princess Alexandra. With two little ones, don't know how she manages but she seems to. Sometimes I wish Suzanne hadn't moved away. Sometimes I feel sure she'd be happier . . . it's just . . . well, she's all on her own in Cricklewood, isn't she?

**Luka**   Alone? She's always out. The pub or parties with her *friends* . . .

**Theresa**   Yes, but what I mean is there's no one special in her life, is there? (*She catches his look.*) Or is there? Is there someone I don't know about? (**Luka** *shakes his head.*) I know

I'm silly and old-fashioned but I just wish she'd meet some nice young man again . . .

**Luka**   A nice young man.

**Theresa**   If there is still such a thing.

**Luka**   My toenail's turning black.

**Theresa**   Did you bang it?

**Luka**   Stubbed it on the bedroom door. Fucking hurt – sorry. Did have them all varnished purple so it wouldn't show.

**Theresa**   You varnish your toenails? I thought only girls did that.

**Luka**   Me too. (*Pause.*) Suzanne did it. Most of it's chipped off now though. (*Pause.*) Mrs Garner . . .

**Theresa**   Yes, dear?

**Luka**   Would you mind if I gave you a bit of advice?

**Theresa**   Oh? No, go ahead – unless it's about painting my nails, I've always thought it looked tarty.

**Luka**   Mrs Garner, if you want to screw that bloke from next door –

**Theresa**   Luka! Oh nonsense, I don't –

**Luka** (*interrupting*)   You've gotta tell him. Tell him or he'll never know. You can't expect him to like read your mind.

**Theresa**   Look, I don't think . . .

**Luka**   He's probably thinking, 'I can't ask her, cos maybe she thinks she's too old for all that. Maybe she'll be like so shocked, she won't want to see me any more, and that's gonna be kinda difficult with living next door and all. I'll have to like creep outside and only take my washing in after dark –'

**Theresa**   Will you stop it?

**Luka**    Tell him. Cook him a nice meal and tell him.

**Theresa**    Risotto.

**Luka**    God, I'm knackered. Got two hours sleep last night on a bench by B&Q.

**Theresa**    You can go to bed if you like. There's a bed made up in the spare room, where you slept at Christmas.

**Luka** (*stands up*)    Thanks. Where'll Suzanne sleep if I have the bed?

*He picks up his trainers.*

**Theresa**    In the double with me. (*She stands, hesitates, then gives him a little kiss on the forehead.*) Goodnight, Luka.

**Luka**    Are you going to wait up for her?

**Theresa**    No . . . Well, actually, I probably will . . . but don't tell her that, will you? It always used to annoy her. When I hear the gate creak, I'll creep upstairs.

**Luka** *exits.* **Theresa** *looks at her watch. She starts to fuss about the room.*


## Scene Three

*The sound of eerily subdued sobbing. A shit-heap of a teenage boy's bedroom.* **Josh**, *in his pyjamas, is asleep sprawled across the split and beer-stained duvet.* **Sophie**, *his younger sister (aged fourteen, also in pyjamas), is trying to rouse him.* **Josh** *wakes.*

**Sophie**    Josh!

**Josh** (*sits up, rubs his nose*)    Shit. (*He looks at* **Sophie**.)

**Sophie** *goes to the top of the bed, pulls the duvet back a bit.* **Suzanne** *is there, crying.*

**Sophie**    Josh! A girl. You've got a girl in here! And she's crying. Why is she crying?

**Josh**    Shit . . .

**Sophie**    Been crying for ages.

**Josh**    Shit.

**Josh** *crawls across to look at* **Suzanne**.

**Sophie**    Thought maybe you'd smuggled another dog in. Not a girl. Fucking hell, Josh.

**Josh**    Shut up. Just shut up, right.

**Sophie**    She can't hear me, she's crying.

**Josh**    I know! (**Suzanne** *curls up, tries to move away.* **Josh** *holds his head.*) My head's fucking killing. . . Like eight beers I had.

**Sophie**    Eight – yeah, right. You'd be dead. Or on a drip like Connor at school, after twelve Bacardi Breezers.

**Josh** *nervously shakes* **Suzanne** *slightly.*

**Sophie**    Hope she don't wake Dad.

**Josh**    Fuck – he's in?

**Sophie**    Yeah. And conscious.

**Josh** (*to* **Suzanne**)    Shhh. Shhhh. Not so loud.

**Sophie**    What did you do to her?

**Josh**    Shit. Fucking hell.

**Sophie**    You must've done something.

**Josh** *gingerly pushes* **Suzanne**'*s shoulder.*

**Sophie**    Did she take anything? Pills? We did like first-aid at school last term.

**Josh**    It's a nightmare.

**Sophie**    You think she's having –

**Josh**    I'm having a nightmare, man.

**Sophie**    Did you fuck her?

**Josh**    Sophie!

**Sophie**    Did you fuck her?

**Josh**    Course I – Oh fuck . . . I hope she's not, you know thinking it was rape or something . . . I mean, she was all over me, fucking ate me alive. Look at these scratches. Shit.

**Sophie**    You didn't hurt her?

**Josh**    Course I didn't . . .

**Sophie**    Not by accident . . . or something.

**Josh**    No . . . least I don't see how.

**Sophie**    You said that Kelly cried. Afterwards, didn't she?

**Josh**    Cos she was crap and I told her so. That's different – And Kelly can't hold her drink.

**Sophie**    Maybe this one can't either. Was it her first time or something . . .

**Josh**    She's not . . . I mean she's . . .

**Sophie**    This is a dangerous situation, right? Maybe we should tell Dad.

**Josh**    Shit! Are you out of your fucking mind? Don't you dare.

**Suzanne** *stops crying*.

**Sophie**    Well, he brings women back and this don't happen.

**Josh**    She's stopped.

**Sophie**    Maybe she's dead.

**Josh** (*he checks on* **Suzanne**)    She's asleep. She was just crying in her sleep.

**Sophie**    Where did you meet her?

**Josh**   The shop.

**Sophie**   You just picked her up? And you're always saying you're too shy. You're outrageous, Josh. Do I know her? From school or anything?

**Josh**   I don't think so, Soph.

**Sophie** (*bending over* **Suzanne**)    Nice perfume. Let me look at her.

**Josh**   No.

**Sophie**   Just her face. I won't wake her. Move the sheet.

**Josh** *moves the sheet, a little, just off* **Suzanne***'s face.*

**Sophie**   Shit! She's a woman! . . . She's like twenty-five or something. Oh my God, Josh.

**Josh**   Shhh.

**Sophie**   A woman . . .

**Josh**   She's beautiful.

**Sophie** (*looks at* **Suzanne** *critically*)    Yeah, I suppose so. Is she naked?

**Josh**   I . . . I can't remember.

**Sophie** *pulls the sheet down, a little, exposing* **Suzanne***'s shoulder.*

**Josh**   Sophie! Leave her.

**Sophie**   I'm just seeing if she's okay.

**Suzanne** *stirs.* **Josh** *and* **Sophie** *jump back,* **Sophie** *cries out,* **Suzanne** *wakes.*

**Suzanne**   Huh? Luka . . .

**Josh**   You were having a bad dream.

**Sophie**   A nightmare.

**Suzanne** *sits up, wide-eyed, startled. Recognition dawns.*

**Josh**   You alright?

**Suzanne**   No.

**Josh**   Fuck . . .

**Suzanne**   Oh no. (*She holds the sheet around herself. She stares at* **Sophie**.) Oh, no, no. (*Pause.*)

**Sophie**   Er, hi. Is everything alright?

**Suzanne** (*confused, to* **Josh**)   This is your place, er. . .

**Josh**   Josh. This is my sister.

**Sophie**   Sophie. (*She holds out her hand. Still slightly dazed, sitting up in bed,* **Suzanne** *shakes it.*) Are you okay?

**Suzanne**   Mmmm.

**Sophie**   Would you like an asprin or anything?

**Suzanne**   Are you . . . ?

**Sophie** *looks at* **Josh** *for help.*

**Josh**   Suzanne . . . last night, do you remember . . . We got a bit wasted? Didn't we? And you wanted to come home with me. You wanted to, didn't you?

**Suzanne**   What? My eyes are burning.

**Sophie**   Cos of all that crying.

**Suzanne**   Crying? What? I'm sorry, I'm still . . . I need a drink . . .

**Josh**   Another one?

**Suzanne**   . . . of water.

**Josh** (*to* **Sophie**)   What're you waiting for? Get the fucking water!

**Sophie** *exits.*

**Suzanne**   Oh my God, look at you. You're a . . . (*She laughs, shocked.*)

**Josh**    And you wanted to come home with me, you wanted to, didn't you?

**Suzanne**    You're a kid . . .

**Josh**    No I'm not.

**Suzanne**    You look like my son. Oh fuck . . . I'm really sorry.

**Josh**    Don't be. It was great.

**Suzanne**    No, no, I don't want to know . . . I shouldn't be here. I must go.

**Suzanne** *gets up, still holding the sheet around herself. She sees her shoes on the floor, and bends to pick them up. She staggers.* **Josh** *helps her sit back down.*

**Josh**    Steady there, take it easy. Everything's okay. Sophie's getting your water.

**Suzanne** (*holds her head*)    Sorry . . . your name . . . ?

**Josh**    Josh.

**Suzanne**    I'm sorry, Josh. I'm really sorry. I don't know what I was thinking of.

**Josh**    You wanted to.

**Suzanne**    It's no excuse.

**Josh**    Just cos I'm young, well, to you, I suppose . . . but I've had lots of girlfriends.

**Suzanne** (*puts her Doc Martens on*)    It's stupid, so stupid . . .

**Josh**    I won't say anything . . . I mean, I fucked my best mate's girlfriend once, kinda by accident. I never let on. Are you like married or anything . . .

**Suzanne**    No. Not now.

**Josh**    But you were? Wow. (*Pause.*) Bet you've got a boyfriend though?

**Suzanne**   Look a sight, don't I?

**Suzanne** *tries to dress discreetly.* **Josh** *turns away.*

**Josh**   If you want me to like wait outside . . .

**Suzanne**   It's okay, love. My knickers . . .

**Josh**   Oh . . . oh yeah. . . (*He looks in the bed and on the floor.*) You can borrow a pair of mine . . . if they'll fit.

**Suzanne**   I woke up . . . looked at you lying there. And I saw my son. The bastards. (*She stands up, clenching her fists, body hard.*) They've got him.

**Josh**   What!

**Suzanne** (*turns on* **Josh**)   My son! They've got my son. Fucking socials.

**Josh**   Social services have like got your kid?

**Suzanne**   My son. They must have. Where else could he be?

*Pause.*

**Josh**   Come on. You better sit down. Come on.

**Suzanne** *wipes her eyes, looks at the make-up on her fingers.*

**Suzanne**   What a night, eh? What a night. I'm sorry. I'm really sorry.

**Josh**   For what?

**Suzanne** (*ruffles his hair*)   And you're so sweet. Really sweet.

**Sophie** *enters with the water.*

**Josh**   At fucking last. Bring it here.

**Sophie** *hands* **Suzanne** *the cup.*

**Suzanne**   What's the time?

**Josh** (*cranes over to look at his clock*)   Seven thirty-four a.m.

**Suzanne**   Oh.

**Sophie**   Shit, my paper round!

**Suzanne** (*to* **Josh**)   Look, love, I ought to be going. Can I use your bathroom?

**Sophie**   Just don't wake Dad.

**Suzanne** *looks at* **Josh**, *alarmed*.

**Josh**   S'alright, he's a heavy sleeper.

**Suzanne** *pauses, unsteady in the doorway.* **Sophie** *joins her.*

**Sophie**   Gonna be long? I need to piss.

**Josh**   Sophie. Let the lady use the bathroom. Use the fucking paper bin.

**Suzanne** *exits.* **Sophie** *tips out the contents of the litter bin, takes it behind the bed.*

**Sophie**   Don't watch, Josh. I'm not gonna piss with you watching.

**Josh** *turns away. Behind the bed,* **Sophie** *squats over the litter bin.*

**Josh**   My nose . . . Does it look really bad?

**Sophie**   Yeah. Is she feeling better?

**Josh**   Social services have got her baby.

**Sophie**   That why she was crying?

**Josh**   We should help her get it back.

**Sophie**   Us?

**Josh**   Someone should help her. She's a beautiful woman, isn't she?

**Sophie** (*pulls back the curtains*)   Shit, it's raining. (*She opens the window, tips the bin of piss out.*)

**Josh**   Mind the fucking begonias.

**Sophie**    Already getting pissed on, ain't they? I'm going to get dressed. See you later.

**Josh**    Sophie, if you say a word to Dad . . .

**Sophie**    Course I won't.

**Suzanne** *enters.*

**Suzanne**    Bathroom's free.

**Sophie**    I'm fine now thanks. See you later.

**Sophie** *exits.*

**Suzanne**    How old's your sister?

**Josh**    Fourteen.

**Suzanne**    And you're . . . ?

**Josh**    Seventeen.

**Suzanne**    Shit.

**Josh**    It's okay.

**Suzanne**    Your sister . . . She wasn't in here earlier when we were . . .

**Josh**    Sophie sleeps in the attic. In a sleeping bag. Got her bedroom too full of computers and stuff.

**Suzanne**    Could I borrow an umbrella? I'll bring it back . . . er, drop it into the shop later.

**Josh**    Look, I could walk you home . . . If you wait a minute while I put some clothes on.

**Suzanne**    Okay.

*She sits back down on the bed.* **Josh** *starts unbuttoning his pyjamas, gets self-conscious, stops.*

**Josh**    There's some cornflakes downstairs. Or toast.

**Suzanne**    I'm fine.

**Josh**    You could make yourself a black coffee . . .

**Suzanne**    Yeah? Yeah, I think I'll do that.

**Suzanne** *exits.* **Josh** *still can't really believe what's happened. Suddenly he grins to himself. He continues to get changed.* **Sophie** *enters with her cycle pads.*

**Sophie**    Lucy's across the road. You know she works at the same place as Dee-Ann now?

**Josh**    Yeah, yeah.

**Sophie** *looks out the window.*

**Sophie**    She's out there doing something to her car. You better take the woman out the side door in case she sees. If Dee-Ann finds out –

**Josh**    Fuck Dee-Ann.

**Sophie**    You can't treat her like that. You've no respect.

**Josh**    You'll understand when you're older.

**Sophie**    I understand now. Men are shits. (*A beat.*) So what about the baby? You're gonna try and help the woman get it back?

**Josh**    Yeah . . . though I don't see how I can do anything . . .

**Sophie**    You're so defeatist, Josh! You could kick up a fuss, go to the papers . . . Oh fuck, I should be like long gone. At least make sure she gets home safely, right?

**Sophie** *exits.*


## Scene Four

**Theresa**'s *kitchen.* **Theresa** *and* **Luka** *are having breakfast.* **Luka** *is reading the paper.* **Theresa** *yawns.*

**Luka**    I didn't sleep either.

**Theresa**    Does Suzanne still drink milk?

**Luka**    Soya milk.

**Theresa**    Oh. Soya milk . . . Made from beans or
something, is it? (*Pause.*) Is she eating properly? I can never
ask her and get a straight answer.

**Luka**    She eats. Then she spews.

**Theresa** (*stops eating*)    She insists she's not bulimic.

**Luka**    Says she's sick cos life makes her feel like that.

**Theresa**    When she was at school she'd be sick every
morning. Once the head sent her home with a letter cos he
thought she was up the club.

**Luka**    She's getting so thin . . .

**Theresa**    I noticed . . .

**Luka**    And she won't see the doctor. Not after she had a
row with her. She just buys all this shit from the health shop
in Kilburn. And then she never takes them.

**Theresa**    Does she cook for you?

**Luka**    If I'm really unlucky. It's okay, cos there's
McDonald's up the road. Course – I don't tell her. But it's
better than like dying of malnutrition.

**Theresa**    When she was little she used to love to help me
in the kitchen, doing the washing-up. Playing with the
bubbles.

**Luka**    Wish she still did.

**Suzanne** *enters*.

**Suzanne** (*coming in*)    Look, sorry, Mum, I . . . (*Sees* **Luka**.)
Oh fuck . . . (**Luka** *gets up*.) Oh my God . . . What the fuck
are you doing down here?

**Luka**    Looking for you, Suzanne.

**Suzanne**    Luka! Shit, you can't imagine. I've been so
worried! What did Joanna have to say?

**Luka**  About what?

**Suzanne**  What do you fucking think?

**Luka**  Nothing.

**Suzanne**  Did you tell her you want to leave?

**Luka**  No, I didn't. Jesus. Suzanne, you're so paranoid. I sat up by B&Q and did some thinking.

**Suzanne**  Then what? You weren't at school in the afternoon. I phoned Marcus.

**Luka**  I went to Pete's, I went round Boris's, I went to the Docket. I was scouring the whole of bloody Cricklewood trying to find you.

**Suzanne**  I stood for 45 minutes outside the fucking playground, I made you food, I went to the arcade.

**Luka**  But what about last night? Where the fuck were you? Your mum waited up all night.

**Theresa**  Well I . . .

**Suzanne**  . . . I've been to a cafe.

**Luka**  You never.

**Theresa**  All night?

**Suzanne**  An all-night cafe. (*To* **Luka**.) But I wouldn't have . . . wouldn't have sat there all night if I'd known you were here. Why didn't you page me?

**Luka**  I was out of my fucking mind, Suzanne. You'd disappeared. Then I get here but you don't come in.

**Theresa**  I thought you might be with your friends.

**Suzanne**  Friends?

**Theresa**  Maria and Michelle.

**Suzanne**  God no. Not seen Michelle for years and Maria's married to a dickhead.

**Theresa**    He seemed alright to me.

**Suzanne**    When did *you* meet him?

**Theresa**    At your wedding.

**Suzanne**    Oh yeah. My wedding. Enough said.

**Theresa**    Do you want some cereal?

**Suzanne**    Just a coffee.

**Theresa** *pours her one.*

**Theresa**    I'm afraid I don't have any soya milk.

**Suzanne**    I'll drink it black.

**Luka**    How many did you have? Coffees in the all-night cafe?

**Suzanne**    Six or seven.

**Theresa**    I'd have thrown up after three.

**Suzanne**    Lightweight.

**Theresa**    They just let you sit there all night?

**Suzanne**    Why shouldn't they? That's what people do in all-night caffs.

**Luka**    You look like you've been doing more than drinking coffee.

**Suzanne** (*sarky*)    Well, yeah, now let me see, I might just've smoked a little crack . . . (**Theresa** *looks at her daughter disapprovingly.* **Suzanne** *sits down next to* **Luka**.) Mum been looking after you has she? (*She ruffles his hair.*)

**Luka**    Get off.

**Suzanne**    When are you gonna do something about your hair?

**Luka**    When are you gonna stop wearing those stupid Doc Martens?

**Suzanne**   You look tired . . .

**Luka**   And whose fault is that?

**Suzanne**   Would you like anything else to eat? Some toast with Marmite.

**Theresa**   I got a new brown loaf . . . Oh . . . Suzanne? What happened to the groceries?

**Suzanne**   Oh fuck! I forgot all about . . . I did buy the stuff for you. Must've left it up the shop.

**Theresa**   You'd lose your head if it wasn't screwed on!

**Suzanne**   It was only three quids worth.

**Theresa**   Still worth checking though, isn't it?

**Suzanne**   Yeah, yeah, leave it to me.

**Luka**   And can you phone school – tell 'em I've like a bad cold or something?

**Suzanne**   Yeah, remind me in a bit. (*She helps herself to a spoonful of* **Luka***'s breakfast.*)

**Theresa**   That's real milk.

**Suzanne** (*to* **Luka**)   So what do you fancy doing? We might as well make a day of it while we're down here. We could go up on the cliffs have a picnic . . .

**Theresa**   Like we used to when you were small. That'd be nice.

**Luka**   I'm still waiting, Suze.

**Suzanne**   Why should I be the one to apologise? It wasn't me who ran away.

**Luka**   I didn't run away. (*Pause.*) Just say sorry, Suzanne.

**Suzanne**   After you had me so worried. You wouldn't answer my messages.

**Luka** *shoves back his chair and stands up.*

**Suzanne**    Oh no. Don't you sulk. (*She tries to put her hand on his shoulder. Angrily he moves aside. Pause.*) Talk to me. Don't you sulk again.

**Theresa**    Leave him be.

**Luka** *tries to pass her.*

**Suzanne**    Don't go walking out on me. (*She blocks his way.*) Look at me. Hey. (*She catches hold of him.*)

**Luka**    I'm not getting into an argument.

**Suzanne**    Then don't give me this silent shit! You know how wound up that makes me.

**Theresa**    Leave him alone, love.

**Suzanne**    Shut up, Mum.

**Theresa**    Don't you start on me.

**Suzanne** (*to* **Luka**)    What is your problem?

**Theresa**    Don't you start/ raising your voice . . .

**Luka**    /Guess. Take a big fucking guess, Suze.

**Suzanne**    Oh it's all my fault, is it? As per usual. Suzanne's gone and fucked/ it all up again, has she!

**Theresa**    /Suzanne! Keep it down. Ned doesn't want to hear this.

**Luka**    Don't you fucking shout at me. Get out of my face.

**Suzanne** *slaps him.*

**Theresa**    Oh/ my God!

**Luka**    /Stupid bitch. You wanna be my mother? Do you? Getting pissed and bringing home psychopaths who want to drink, beat her up and get her kids put in care . . .

**Theresa**    Luka –

**Luka**    You wanna hit me over the head with my skateboard?

**Theresa** *stands up but isn't sure what to do.*

**Luka**   You are just like my mother. You drink more than she does, you smoke more dope than she does . . . Just like her but with one big difference. One really big difference.

**Suzanne**   Luka, listen to me.

**Luka**   I don't give a shit where you were, okay? You're just so fucking immature. Can't keep a job, so you think looking after fucked-up kids is easier./ 'Stability', that's what they said I needed. Stability.

**Theresa**   /Stop this. Please, Luka!

**Suzanne**   It wasn't me that ran. You always run. That's what the socials said.

**Luka**   I came to find you! I thought you were cutting your wrists or under a fucking train or something.

**Suzanne**   None of the others were trouble like you. They warned me . . .

**Luka**   And you didn't listen . . . Didn't care cos you looked at me and you thought –

**Suzanne**   I thought I could help you have a better life.

**Luka**   In your shitty flat?/ Like no one bothered to ask me what I wanted.

**Theresa**   /I'm not gonna put up with this.

**Suzanne**   So what did you want?/ The fucking earth as usual?

**Luka**   An old foster-mum, so there'd be no confusion, y'know. I wouldn't start forgetting what she was there for.

**Suzanne**   Luka!

**Luka** (*he realises* **Theresa** *is present*)   A rich foster-mum. One who'd give me twenty quid a week pocket money – not force to me go out and get a job . . .

**Suzanne**  Force you to get a job? You came home and told me you were working at the all-night garage.

**Luka**  Yeah, cos I need to live, I need money . . .

**Theresa**  Is anyone listening to me?

**Suzanne**  And where'm I supposed to get it?

**Luka**  You could get a job, 'stead of sitting around on your fucking arse. I didn't want to live in another rubbish flat . . . so my mum has to look after my dog till we move, then we don't move and she kidnaps her.

**Suzanne**  We'll get Scully back, I told you –

**Theresa**  That poor little puppy . . .

**Luka**  Yeah, you told me. Told me you'd stop going out, stop holding stupid parties, stop hanging with your stupid friends . . . I thought my socials had like lined up this rich family and then I end up in your skanky flat with you going fucking crazy on me.

**Suzanne**  You think the rich people would've put up with you? Think they'd mind you setting their carpet on fire?

**Luka**  Rich people don't have carpet, Suzanne. And it was an accident, right? I only started using paper cups as ash trays cos you did. Then you like total the fucking car . . .

**Suzanne**  So I can't even write off my own car/ without you judging me.

**Theresa**  /You've had an accident?

**Luka**  I'm a better driver than you and I ain't had any proper lessons./ When I take my test I'll pass first time. How many goes did it take you? Eleven? Eleven, Suze.

**Theresa**  /Oh my God.

**Suzanne**  I drove you everywhere – I was your fucking taxi service. I put myself out for you. I cook, I clean . . .

**Theresa**  /Suzanne . . .

**Luka**   Where? Where do you cook and clean? Not in our fucking flat, that's for sure.

**Suzanne**   And . . . and . . . when the school caught you truanting, I said I'd kept you home –

**Luka**   And you want a medal for it? When some guy at school was bad-mouthing you, saying you look like a slag, I split his face. Even though now him and his mates are like just waiting their chance to cut my guts out.

**Theresa**   Honestly, I've completely had it/ with you two.

**Suzanne**   /What do you want? Do you want to leave me? Do you?

*Pause.*

**Theresa**   I'm sure he doesn't want that dear, he –

**Suzanne**   Shut up.

**Theresa**   I won't/ shut up in my own home . . .

**Suzanne** (*to* **Luka**)   /You can leave me, can't you? Any time you want. It's easy enough. It's not working out, you can go, can't you?

**Luka**   I just want you to change, Suze.

**Suzanne**   Into an old rich woman who pays for you to have driving lessons?

**Luka**   I just don't want to have to look out for you the whole time, I don't want the responsibility.

**Suzanne**   Alright, okay. I'll change. I'll change into somebody else. I'll be what you want me to be.

**Luka**   You always say that. You don't change. You can't.

**Suzanne**   And like you're perfect, are you? The perfect foster-son. Never give me a moment's fucking worry, do you!

**Luka**   Just . . . just get out of my life, bitch.

**Theresa**  Well, honestly . . .

**Luka** *exits*.

**Suzanne**  Yeah, go and sulk. Like you always do.

**Theresa** *puts the kettle on again*.

**Suzanne**  What're you looking looking at?

**Theresa**  I'm not saying any more.

**Suzanne**  Like you're the perfect mother . . .

*Pause*.

You don't have to live with him.

**Theresa**  Neither do you if it's not working.

**Suzanne**  It's not his fault. He's had a hard time . . . and he's at that age where he thinks he knows it all.

**Theresa**  You were like that. And still are.

**Suzanne**  If I'm fucked up, it's how you made me. You and Dad.

**Theresa**  We stayed together for your sake.

**Suzanne**  And made us all fucking miserable.

**Theresa**  If you didn't swear so much, at least you'd be setting that boy some kind of example.

**Suzanne**  So what? Luka and me – we swear and spit and scream, so what? We've got a lot to be pissed off about.

**Theresa**  You don't know when you're well off.

**Suzanne**  Well off! Why don't you ever listen to yourself, Mum?

**Theresa**  You've got a roof over your heads.

**Suzanne**  Have you seen it? My roof? No you haven't. You haven't cos it's four floors up and there's two more of them floors between it and me. One with a demented cow who plays her fucking Steps CDs all night and the other with a mad bloke who leaves his windows open and screams blue murder, night and day.

**Theresa**   You should move.

**Suzanne**   Yeah right. Go down the estate agents and say 'Yeah I'll have that one – the nice semi, with conservatory and reception rooms.' What the fuck's a reception room? I even went and got a job, Mum. You'd think I'd have learnt by now, wouldn't you? Course I lost my benefits, and no contract, no minimum wage, but what use are fucking A levels anyway? So there I am in a City coffee bar, making coffees, all kinds of bloody coffees – as quick as possible. And you've got to make them just right – just a drop to much milk and a macchiato becomes a latte and you can bet your life the customer's gonna give you hell. First day I scald my wrist so bad the skin just peeled off like it was plaster. The supervisor says I'm working too slow, starts standing right behind me . . . and pressing his fucking little dick against my arse. I tell him he's looking to get a Premium Expresso burning his beans. And if it wasn't him, it was the hordes of City tossers, trying to tug my thong every time I reached over to wipe a table. But I put up with the verbal, the groping cos I needed the money, needed to move from that shitty flat. Then Joanna says Luka's not going to school. 'Maybe you should try to be there for him a little more', or 'Maybe his needs don't fit in with your new career.' 'Career', yeah that was their word – my coffee-making career. So I cut down my hours, and then it wasn't worth the tube fare in.

**Theresa**   Perhaps after Luka's moved on –

**Suzanne**   Moved on? He's not moving on.

**Theresa**   I mean later on . . . You'll have the chance to get a better job using your A levels –

**Suzanne**   No one wants my fucking A levels. If you've never had anything but shit jobs. you'll never get anything but shit jobs. You know that, if anyone does.

**Theresa**   I enjoyed my job . . .

**Suzanne**   Even though it's left you doubled up with sciatica and blind as a bat.

**Theresa**   It was the people . . . being with the other girls, having a gossip and a giggle. Plus we got the seconds cut-price, and halfway decent knickers aren't cheap. It was the friendship. That's where you miss out. I think you're a bit isolated in London really . . .

**Suzanne**   I've got my friends and in the end it's been one kid after another. With some, like Stefan, I had no free time at all. Take my eyes off him for two minutes and he'd be cutting his wrists.

**Theresa**   I just think . . . it'd be nice if you met someone again. Someone special.

**Suzanne**   Special? Oh I've met some really special guys, Mum.

**Theresa**   Maybe you're just not looking in the right place.

**Suzanne**   I'm not looking at all. They find me. Like fleas find a fucking dog.

**Theresa**   You just need someone nice . . .

**Suzanne**   Nice like Andy?

**Theresa**   You were in love. You were, Suzanne.

**Suzanne**   When he saw me struggling to pitch my tent, came to help and made a complete fucking cack of it cos he was so stoned, I thought he was wildest man at Glastonbury. Two years later he's like software sales bore of the century. I'm waking up next to Mr Floppy Disk and wanting to press eject.

**Theresa**   And now there's no one?

**Suzanne**   Not at the moment, no. I'm picky. Shame you weren't a bit more picky yourself.

**Theresa**   If you mean your father . . . we weren't so badly suited . . . we made the best of what we had till the last few years.

**Suzanne**   Even if that wasn't very much.

**Theresa**   If he hadn't had that crash, and hit his head . . . if that hadn't changed him . . .

**Suzanne**   Well thank fuck for black ice.

**Theresa**   Suzanne! (*Pause.*) Look, don't jump down my throat, but have you ever thought at all about joining a dating agency?

**Suzanne**   You're a loopy old bag sometimes.

**Theresa**   Think you'll always be young?

**Suzanne**   I'm not young, Mum. (*Pause.*) So what about this picnic then? A picnic at Beachy Head.

**Theresa**   I didn't think you were very –

**Suzanne**   Come on. Are you gonna get ready? Put your best frock on like you always used to, so you can get grass stains and dog shit on it and moan all the way home. We should buy a football on the way. And have you still got my kite? Let's take the kite.

**Theresa**   I . . . I gave it to Help the Aged.

**Suzanne**   Fucking hell.

**Theresa**   It'd got the moth anyway. But I think we've got a football . . . And I could make some sandwiches if you do really want to go . . . cucumber sarnies. . .

**Suzanne** (*runs from the room, to shout up the stairs*)   Luka! Luka, we're going for a picnic!

**Luka** (*shouts down*)   Fuck you!

## Scene Five

*The shop.* **Josh** *is at his counter.* **Sophie** *is lounging in the doorway, playing a Craig David CD on her stereo.*

**Sophie**   It's a cool job, bro. Well, at least you don't have to wear a poncey uniform, like Calum does at the Co-op. And you don't have a boss breathing down your neck most of the time.

**Josh**   Yeah, but how long before they catch him out?

**Sophie**   How can he spend his whole life in the bookies? That is so like totally irresponsible.

**Josh**   All this standing around is . . . I don't know . . . it's starting to bug me.

**Sophie**   You get to read all the magazines. You can just stand there looking at Gail Porter in a thong and get paid for it.

**Josh**   Badly paid for it.

**Sophie**   So why don't you leave school then? Get a full-time job . . . though nobody'll pay you very much cos you're not interested in anything that pays.

**Josh**   It's not just computer programmers that get rich, Soph. But I wasn't talking about leaving school – just getting a job with more social hours. When I think I could be out there . . . 3.07 on a Friday and I'm going to be here till half eleven . . . My life's drifting away.

**Sophie**   Girls come in sometimes . . .

**Josh**   When you're not standing in the doorway, squeezing your spots.

**Sophie**   Fuck you. And you met that woman last night.

**Josh**   I told you that's like a non-subject.

**Sophie**   Yeah but –

**Josh**   A non-subject.

**Sophie** You think she'll come in again today? (*Pause.*) A quid says she won't. (*Pause.*) You really want to see her again, don't you? Your older lady. (*Pause.*) She's got a kid she said. She's probably like married.

**Josh** She's divorced. Anyway, I'm not discussing it.

**Luka** *enters, approaching the shop.*

**Josh** Shit. It's the homicidal hedgehog killer.

**Sophie** You what?

**Josh** A psycho, Sophie. If he comes in, don't look at him, right? Avoid eye contact.

**Luka** *comes in.* **Sophie** *looks intently at her stereo.* **Luka** *walks up to the counter.*

**Luka** Did my mum leave some shopping here last night? (**Josh** *stares at him.*) About three quid's worth. It'll be in two carrier bags, one inside the other, cos she always thinks they're gonna split.

**Josh** Oh . . .

**Luka** *wanders to the fridge, takes a can of Red Bull.*

**Josh** The police are looking for you. This shop takes assault on its employees very seriously.

**Luka** Come here.

**Josh** I'll press the panic button.

**Luka** Have you got the shopping or not?

**Josh** I have . . . but you see, there's a rule . . . there's a rule, isn't there, Sophie?

**Sophie** Like how would I know?

**Luka** *looks at* **Sophie**, *she looks at him.*

**Josh** The customer has to sign for the goods in person.

**Luka** I can do her signature.

**Josh** (**Luka** *looks under the counter*)　It's not there. It's in the safe.

**Luka**　I can do her signature.

**Josh**　There's like this alarm on the safe, isn't there, Sophie?

**Sophie**　Uhuh.

**Luka** *looks at* **Sophie**.

**Josh**　It alerts the police.

**Luka**　Your nose looks like shit, man. Like a fucking squashed tomato. (*He wanders to the door, walks past* **Sophie**.) Want Craig David to fill you in, huh? (*He beckons to someone off outside. Shouts.*) Mum! The kid says you've gotta like come in and sign for it. Turn the fucking stereo down. (**Sophie** *does*.) Not you, Sweetness. (*To* **Suzanne**, *off.*) Turn the fucking car stereo down, if you can't hear me.

**Luka** *exits.* **Sophie** *goes to* **Josh**.

**Sophie**　Do you know him?

**Josh**　It was him that gave me this. (*He indicates his nose.*)

**Sophie** (*a little impressed*)　Yeah?

**Suzanne** *enters in a summer dress (and still wearing those DMs.)* **Josh** *is visibly affected.*

**Josh** (*to* **Sophie**)　Beat it, Soph.

**Sophie**　Josh . . .

**Josh**　Disappear.

**Sophie** (*smiles at* **Suzanne**)　Hi ya. (*She saunters off among the shelves.*)

**Josh**　I'll . . . just get your shopping.

**Josh** *scurries off to the back of the shop.* **Suzanne** *picks up a bag of jelly babies, then goes behind the counter to take a packet of cigarettes. She hesitates, then pockets them. She looks at the front of her dress,*

*hesitates, checks* **Josh**'s *not watching and puts them down her front.*
**Josh** *comes back with* **Suzanne**'s *shopping.*

**Suzanne**    Your nose looks like shit.

**Josh**    Thanks. (*Pause.*) He . . . he's your son?

**Suzanne**    Foster-son.

**Josh**    Oh.

**Suzanne**    Does this pay?

**Josh**    What?

**Suzanne**    I oughta try and get another job. (*She presses a couple of buttons on the till.*) Oh, how does this one open?

**Josh** (*smiling*)    Are you gonna rob it? (*She smiles.*) It's like this. (*He opens the till.*)

**Suzanne**    Yeah, like in the coffee shop. That's what I used to do. Sell coffee. Boring as shit. I wouldn't mind working in a pet shop . . . or a florist maybe. Arranging bunches of flowers for people, that would keep you cheerful, wouldn't it?

**Josh**    And wreaths for funerals?

**Suzanne**    Oh yeah, that'd be a bit of a downer. What about a CD shop?

**Josh**    They're still called record shops.

**Suzanne**    Thanks, Mr Fucking Know-all. How can they call it a record shop if it only sells CDs? Whatever happened to trade descriptions? I just gotta find some kind of job. Something that's not all stress or heavy lifting. You sell books in here?

**Josh** (*gestures to a rack*)    Bargain ones. Shite mostly.

**Suzanne**    Is there any of those 'Change Your Life' ones?

**Josh**    There's one on learning to look into the future, I think. We've had that for years.

**Suzanne**   I don't want to know about the future, not at the moment. Not till I've done something about making things right for him.

**Josh**   Him?

**Suzanne** (*gestures towards the door*)   Him.

*Uneasy pause.* **Josh** *goes back to the till, closes it.*

**Suzanne**   I paid you last night, didn't I?

**Josh**   What? Yeah. You did. (*He hands her the shopping.*) Suzanne. (*Pause.*) Can I see you again?

**Suzanne**   No. No, I don't think so.

*A car horn. She hesitates. Then leans over the counter to kiss* **Josh**. *She means it just to be a little one, but it doesn't work out that way. They part.* **Suzanne** *exits.*

**Sophie** (*looks out from behind the shelf*)   Wow.

**Josh**   Shut it.

**Sophie**   Romance. He's blushing. Got an erection?

**Josh**   Don't you have some place to go?

**Sophie**   He has. He's hiding it behind the counter. (*She goes to the window.*) Crap car they've got.

**Josh**   Get away from the fucking window.

**Sophie**   There was a message for you on the machine. From Dee-Ann.

**Josh**   Right.

**Sophie**   You've so many girls, Josh. Such a *stud*.

**Josh**   Just fuck off right?

**Sophie**   I could tell 'em some stuff about you – like that you have to spray your trainers with deodorant, and you never clean your teeth . . .

**Josh**   You're such a child, Sophie.

**Sophie**  Just cos you've been to bed with a *woman*. (*A beat.*) But you can't really go out with her if she's that guy's mum, can you?

**Josh**  She's not his real mum.

**Sophie**  She's loads too old for you anyway. And she didn't say she wants to see you again –

**Josh**  When I want advice I won't ask a fucking virgin.

**Sophie**  What makes you think I'm still . . .

**Josh**  Because nobody'd ball a spotty geek girl.

**Sophie**  I'm not spotty. Okay, it was a problem, but I tackled it.

**Josh**  Fuck, you sound exactly like Mum sometimes.

**Sophie**  Better than sounding like Dad.

**Josh**  Why don't you go back to live at Mum's?

**Sophie**  Just so you can take over my bedroom? I ain't having you in there. And I've passworded the whole system now.

**Josh**  Like I'm oh-so-interested in American boys who e-mail and tell you they look like Brad Pitt. Like Brad Pitt after his billionth burger.

**Sophie**  He's not the only guy I chat on-line with. There's Cody, who's from Tampa, and he scanned in these pics of him surfing . . .

**Josh**  So why don't you piss off to America then?

**Sophie**  I might do. I might go to college there or something.

**Josh**  Yeah, right.

**Sophie**  Mr James says I could.

**Josh**  Swot.

**Sophie**   You only think that's an insult cos you're so under-motivated, Josh. Swot is the new cool.

**Josh** (*not convinced*)   Yeah, right.

**Sophie**   The thing is to stay focused. That's what Mr James says.

**Josh**   Did him a lot of good, didn't it? Teaching at our school – he's really got a long way in the world. You're a dreamer. You're beyond help, Josh.

**Josh**   Dee-Ann had ambitions. And what is she? A secretary.

**Sophie**   At least she's got keyboard skills. She can build on those later if she wants to . . .

**Josh**   'Build on those later' – hallo, it's the mobile careers lesson, coming to a convenience store near you.

**Sophie**   You've just got to make the most of your opportunities, haven't you? (*A beat.*) What're you gonna do if Dee-Ann finds out about the woman?

**Josh**   She won't.

**Sophie**   I'm saying what if she does?

**Josh**   I'll finish with her.

**Sophie**   The woman?

**Josh**   Dee-Ann.

**Sophie**   I can see all kinds of problems, if you get involved with the woman.

**Josh**   Yeah, well, why don't you go on *Jerry Springer* and tell everyone all about it?

**Sophie**   It'll all end in tears, Josh . . .

**Josh**   Yeah, yeah, just cos you can't get laid.

**Sophie**   It's not you she wants, she's just desperate for it.

**Josh**   What?

**Sophie**   Women need sex more as they get old. I read a survey.

**Josh**   She's not *old*. And she's not desperate. It's no good talking to you, you won't understand.

**Josh** *takes a beer from the fridge, opens and swigs from it.*

**Sophie**   Drinking the stock again. (*Pause.*) Look, just admit it's never gonna work out. You and the woman.

**Josh**   Her name is Suzanne.

**Sophie**   I'm just saying it won't work, so it's no good getting in a state about it.

**Josh**   I'm not getting in a state about anything.

**Sophie**   You're drinking and it's not even four o'clock. (*Pause.*) Why did he hit you? Her foster-son.

*He swigs the beer.*

You'll end up an old piss-head like Dad.

**Josh**   Oh just fuck off out of it, Soph. Go and bother someone else. Go back to your lardy yanks on the Internet. (*He walks off among the shelves, still drinking.*) I've work to do.

**Sophie** (*turns to leave*)   Fine. Enjoy your life in Loser-ville.

**Sophie** *exits.*


**Scene Six**

**Suzanne** *is sitting on the grass, looking at the view.*

*Enter* **Luka** (*carrying a football*). *He flops down beside her.*

**Suzanne**   I think Ned must spend half his life polishing that car. I mean what for? It's not as if it's even a new one.

**Luka**   Shame you didn't clean your car occasionally. Or empty the rubbish out of it.

**Suzanne**   Life's too short for that.

*She lies down.*

Come here. Be my pillow.

*She uses **Luka**'s chest as a pillow.*

**Luka**   Don't start talking about the clouds.

**Suzanne**   Why?

**Luka**   You always say look at that one, doesn't it look like this or that. When it just looks like a fucking cloud.

**Suzanne**   I thought you liked me talking about the clouds.

**Luka**   Well now you know I don't, don't you?

*Pause. He strokes her hair. She relaxes a bit.*

**Suzanne**   I'd like to move back down here. Are you listening?

*Pause.*

Would you like to live down here?

*Pause.*

Would you?

**Luka**   I don't care.

**Suzanne**   If I did, right? Moved back to Brighton. Would you come? Or would you want to stay near your brother and sister?

**Luka**   And my friends. Marcus, Tariq.

**Suzanne**   You'd rather I didn't move then?

**Luka**   I didn't say that.

*He moves away from under her.*

**Luka**   It's up to you Suzanne. You do what you wanna do. I don't know what I want. It's complicated.

**Suzanne**   I want to be with you.

*He squirms back beneath her so she's leaning on him again.*

**Luka**    You are.

*Pause.*

It's not good just like moving somewhere else and thinking things'll be different. I mean you move from your shitty little flat to a shitty little flat down here . . . so what? What's gonna change? How're things suddenly gonna be like wonderful? I don't get it.

**Suzanne**    Maybe a change would . . . change things.

**Luka**    What about getting a caravan? Be better than living in a flat.

**Suzanne**    You want us to become traverllers?

**Luka**    I mean a caravan in a caravan park. A big one with a proper loo and shower.

**Suzanne**    In a caravan park all your neighbours are old.

**Luka**    But you don't share walls with nobody – so you could play the Chili Peppers all night. Leave the door open and dance in the fields.

**Suzanne**    Dance in the fields . . . That'd be so cool.

**Luka**    But not in those fucking boots.

**Suzanne**    Okay, so I'll rent us a caravan. Down here? Or where?

**Luka**    It's only a dream. You take everything so seriously.

*Pause.*

**Suzanne**    Things are serious, Luka. More serious than you can know.

*She reaches back to feel where he is.*

Where are yer?

*She touches his leg.*

**Luka**    Don't.

**Suzanne**    Why?

**Luka**   You know why.

**Suzanne**   No I don't.

**Luka**   They'll come over with the picnic, and I'll be lying here with my dick pointing straight at the clouds.

**Suzanne**   Now who's talking about clouds.

**Luka**   Like pardon me a minute Mr Bisset, while my foster-mum sucks me off.

**Suzanne**   When I wanted you to call me Mum you wouldn't.

**Luka**   Sorry, Mum.

*She gets up.*

**Suzanne**   Don't.

**Luka**   What? What is it? Mum.

**Suzanne**   I've been trying to pick my moment . . . or maybe I've been trying to avoid it. . . . Fuck it, there's never gonna be a right moment.

**Luka** *gets up, starts kicking the football around.*

**Luka**   A right time to tell me what? You love me? I know, I know. Say 'I love you motherfucker'.

**Suzanne** *kicks the ball violently away.*

**Theresa** (*off* )   Suzanne. Don't leave us to carry the whole picnic.

**Suzanne** (*to* **Luka**)   I'm having your baby.

*Pause.*

**Luka**   Wow.

*He stares at her. Pause.*

**Suzanne**   Is that all you're gonna say?

**Luka**   Yeah. Yeah it is. Shit

*Blackout.*

# Act Two

## Scene One

*Beachy Head.*

*After the picnic. The picnic cloth is spread with paper plates and other debris.*

**Ned** *and* **Theresa** *are sitting on the grass, looking up at the sky.* **Ned** *wears sunglasses, and has his map with him.* **Theresa** *is in a summer dress and cardi.*

**Theresa**    I can hear a lark but I can't see him.

**Ned**    There. Look.

**Theresa**    Can't see a bleedin' thing. Your eyes are much better than mine. Too many years squinting over a sewing machine. (*To* **Ned**.) We'd always come up here with the kids in the summer. A car full of little boys. Even Suzanne's friends were mostly boys. We'd set up cricket stumps, play rounders . . . I could never hit the bloody ball . . . Did you ever used to come up here?

**Ned**    Once or twice maybe. We used to play cricket on Beach Green. You know, along by Goring.

**Theresa**    Of course, you were living out that way when yours were small. A bit of a long drive out here wasn't it?

**Ned**    And Helen was nervous of heights.

**Theresa**    Was she? I thought you used to go mountaineering.

**Ned**    No. Hill walking.

**Theresa** (*laughing*)    I used to imagine the pair of you scaling the heights with ropes and what are those things? Crampons? I used to think you were so intrepid.

**Ned** (*smiling*)    Well, I'm sorry to disappoint you.

**Theresa**   Hill walking sounds nice though. Where'd you go?

**Ned**   Oh all over. The Pennines, Cumbria. North Wales . . .

**Theresa** (*laughing*)   Anywhere with hills basically? I wish we'd had a hobby like that – something we could do together as a family . . . Your three must've loved it.

**Ned**   Well . . . they did when they were very small . . . Later the girls'd rather go to a holiday camp – for the discos mainly, I think, and then it was 'why can't we go to Lanzarote, Dad?'

**Theresa**   But Michael, he must've loved it . . .

**Ned**   He was never an outdoors type really. Always whining that his feet hurt, he was cold or something had bitten him.

**Theresa**   Still it was doing them good. All in the fresh air.

*Slightly awkward pause. She offers him a jelly baby from the packet.*

**Ned**   No thanks.

**Theresa**   Not got much of a sweet tooth, have you? I'm glad the map of Dunoon was worth having.

**Ned**   It's in really good condition too.

**Theresa**   Where exactly is Dunoon? Can I see?

**Ned**   I'm not going to open it until we get back. You have to handle them so carefully, make sure you don't damage the folds.

*She handles it gingerly, it's in a clear polythene enevelope.*

Ellis Martin's one of my favourite illustrators. He often featured a car like this and used his family as models. Must of been a nice day out for them while he was painting. Little works of art his map covers were – mini masterpieces for three shillings.

**Theresa**   Maps aren't something you ever chuck away are they? You always think you'll go back to a place, even if you never do.

*Enter* **Suzanne** *and* **Luka**.

**Suzanne**    Ow! Something's stung me. Look.

**Theresa** *shares a smile with* **Ned**. **Suzanne** *and Luka flop down.*

**Luka**    It's nettle rash.

**Suzanne**    No, it fucking hurts. Look, Mum.

**Suzanne** *rubs her leg.* **Luka** *slaps her hand off it.*

**Theresa**    I can't see anything.

**Suzanne**    You might if you wore your bloody glasses.

**Theresa**    Can't see with 'em, can't see without 'em.

**Suzanne**    Well you need a new pair don't you?

**Theresa**    Can't afford 'em can I? Not every couple of years.

**Ned**    They do some quite good two-pairs-for-the-price-of-one offers now.

**Theresa**    Be alright if I could afford the one pair to start with.

**Theresa** *stands up.*

Well I don't know about you lot, but I could do with a bit of a stroll, after all that food.

**Ned**    We could walk up as far as the lighthouse.

**Ned** *gets up and goes with her.* **Luka** *and* **Suzanne** *watch them leave.*

*Exit* **Ned** *and* **Theresa** *(or walk along cliff edge).*

**Suzanne**    You're so . . . I don't know . . . philosophical about it. I'd been going crazy wondering whether to tell you . . . trying to imagine what you'd say.

*Pause.*

I was scared you'd leave me.

**Luka**    It's one of those things . . . that's both good and bad at once.

**Suzanne**    Can you imagine what it's gonna be like, being a dad?

**Luka**    Pushing a three-wheeled buggy down the Broadway? Unless you move back down here that is.

**Suzanne**    I move? Not we move?

**Luka**    We move. As long as it's a caravan, not a shitty flat.

**Suzanne**    I don't know how it happened . . .

**Luka** (*sarkily*)    Really?

**Suzanne**    I should've been more careful . . . I mean I never got pregnant by my husband, so I thought –

**Luka**    Was he shite at sex?

**Suzanne**    No, no . . . it was okay.

**Luka**    I'm better than okay aren't I?

**Suzanne**    Yes dear.

**Luka**    Three times a night. I'm superb.

**Suzanne**    Wait 'til you're thirty.

**Luka**    I'll keep fit. Keep in practise. (*Pause.*) Were you faithful? To randy Andy?

**Suzanne** (*looking away – i.e. lying*)    Yeah.

**Luka**    I don't think I could be.

**Suzanne**    You're young.

**Luka**    You don't like it when I look at girls.

**Suzanne**    Can't stop you though, can I?

**Luka**    Nope.

**Suzanne**    I wish I was still sixteen.

**Luka**    I wish I was your age.

**Suzanne**   Do you? It's not much fun.

*Pause.*

I know you say you fancied me from day one, but I didn't have any inkling. Didn't feel it. It wasn't until you had a friend from school round – that girl with the short black bob . . .

**Luka**   Melissa?

**Suzanne**   . . . And the big nose . . .

**Luka**   Melissa.

**Suzanne**   You were flirting with her. . . Sitting on the sofa watching *Gladiator* I was shocked to realise I was jealous. But I still think nothing would've happened . . . I'd have been able to fight it . . . if I hadn't got wasted at Boris's birthday and you hadn't had to put me to bed. Why didn't you go to your own bed?

**Luka**   You wouldn't shut up, you kept going, 'Stay here', 'Don't leave me'.

**Suzanne**   Yeah, but the next morning . . . you woke up with a –

**Luka** (*interrupts*)   Weren't nobody's fault. It just happened.

**Suzanne**   I still feel kind of maternal towards you. I know it's fucked up but there it is.

**Luka**   I'd be in trouble if people knew?

**Suzanne**   You wouldn't. I would.

**Luka**   I know you would. You're a very bad girl.

**Suzanne**   I'd leave the country.

**Luka**   To go where?

**Suzanne**   I don't know. Somewhere warm. Brazil.

**Luka**    I wouldn't let you. I don't want my baby growing up in Brazil. (*Pause.*) You'll have to stop drinking and smoking, Suze.

**Suzanne**    This is my last spliff.

**Luka**    You're getting our kid stoned.

**Suzanne**    It's not big enough yet. This is my last boozing session.

**Luka**    You'll have to wear tent dresses.

**Suzanne**    I will not. I'm not gonna be that big.

**Luka**    You should tell your mum. I don't mean tell her it's mine – just tell her.

**Suzanne**    Make up a boyfriend?

**Luka**    Say he's someone you're not seeing anymore. Same as you'll tell the socials.

**Suzanne**    They won't suspect anything will they?

**Luka**    Course not.

**Suzanne**    You sure you won't just let it slip out?

**Luka**    I'm not stupid. I tell 'em as little as possible about my life y'know. I'm the least of their worries. I mean there's other guys Joanna has to deal with doing all kinds of shit.

**Suzanne**    Joanna's always been really friendly to me. Sometimes I almost forget and want to tell her things.

**Luka**    She says 'How're you finding things at Suzanne's? Is that still working out for you.' I go 'Fine, yes', she goes 'Is there anything you want to talk about?' and I'm like 'No'. That's how you gotta be.

**Suzanne**    When you're eighteen, I guess we can be open about things if we want.

**Luka**    We'll probably have another two kids by then.

**Suzanne**   We fucking won't! I'm going back on the pill.
The extra strong variety.

**Luka**   Yeah and you're going out to work. I don't want
my baby living in your crummy flat. You gotta afford to live
somewhere nice.

**Suzanne**   What about you?

**Luka**   I've already got a job.

**Suzanne**   A Saturday job.

**Luka**   Friday night and Saturday – 45 quid I bring in.
You should work, Suze. What's the problem with that?
We'd have some money – for nice stuff for the baby. You
could get another office job. You've experience.

**Suzanne**   It's all changed though. I was just doing filing.
Now it's all on computer. And I don't know one end of a
computer from t'other.

**Luka**   I can show you. We can get one.

**Suzanne**   If we could afford it.

**Luka**   I won't be poor like you. I'm gonna make a success
of myself. Run a business. Sell mobile phones or something.
I saw a bloke who'd done that on *Working Breakfast*. He was
raking it in.

**Suzanne**   You see me as a failure, don't you?

**Luka**   No . . . not really.

**Suzanne**   How're you gonna become a businessman?
Without money?

**Luka**   I'll go to college.

**Suzanne**   It didn't get me anywhere.

**Luka**   Maybe you took the wrong things then. Took
exams in things nobody wants.

**Suzanne**    It's people like us nobody wants. Look at people in top jobs – are they like us? Do you actually know anyone in a top job?

**Luka**    I've met my social worker's boss. He's got a Mercedes. Tariq's brother plays for QPR.

**Suzanne**    I'm not saying you shouldn't be ambitious. When I came out of college I really tried. I didn't know exactly what I wanted to do . . . work in a museum or an art gallery, that would've been nice. Looking after the exhibitions and answering people's questions. But there's only one museum in Brighton and they didn't want me. Got taken on at the Inland Revenue. A rewarding career, they said. But when I asked about promotion it was 'Oh we don't need any more administrators right now.' You couldn't even get to the second rung. To get to the top you needed to come in much higher up. Unless you can afford to go to university you're fucked. I did apply for jobs where they ask for A levels but didn't get past the interview. You're up against the posh kids – dressed up to the nines, taught to be confident and how to behave in interviews. You don't stand a chance . . .

*Pause.*

If I can do anything to help you get a good a start in business I will – anything.

**Luka**    Have you been thinking about names? It's really important we pick something good. Nothing embarrassing.

**Suzanne**    I've not really started to think . . . of it as a him or a her.

**Luka**    Well, you got to.

**Suzanne**    I'm still finding it difficult to believe.

**Luka**    The doctor's certain?

**Suzanne**    Yeah, I know it's for real . . . I just don't feel . . . like a proper mother. I know I've fostered a few kids, but Stefan was twelve, Carl eleven, even little Zoe was nine. I felt more like . . . a big sister I suppose . . . That's how I saw you to begin with . . . like a younger brother really.

**Luka** While I'm at college, if we move back down here your mum can look after the baby. Your mum and Mr Bisset.

**Suzanne** That's not gonna work out.

**Luka** She must like babies, she brought up you and your brothers, didn't she?

**Suzanne** I mean her and Mr Bisset's not gonna work out.

**Luka** Give 'em a chance. Why don't you think it'll work?

**Suzanne** He's nice. I like him . . . But I think they're both very different.

**Luka** So?

**Suzanne** I think he still misses his wife. Like big time.

*Pause.* **Luka** *gets up, plays with the football.*

**Luka** Scully would love it up here. I'm gonna get her back. Even if I have to go and like break in to me mum's when she's out.

**Suzanne** When your mum rang up, I told her I'd sue her if she didn't give her back.

**Luka** It's too slow. I've had enough with courts. It's pathetic. Mum never takes Scully out, never fucking walks her. Just leaves her to shit in the garden then sticks flower pots over it.

**Suzanne** Your mum could do with the exercise.

**Luka** Fat bitch. You're gonna be a fat bitch too, soon.

**Suzanne** Fuck off.

**Luka** And don't swear in front of the baby.

**Suzanne** (*suddenly jumps up*) Mum! Get away from the edge!

**Theresa** (*off*)    I'm not at the edge.

**Suzanne**    Famous last words. It can crumble, you know. Lots of people have been caught out and gone over. (*To* **Luka**.) Dozy old cow.

**Luka**    Can you like survive it?

**Suzanne**    Only if you get stuck on a ledge or something. If it breaks your fall. I suppose as Mr Bisset's a mountaineer he could rescue her.

**Luka**    Thought he was a coach driver.

**Suzanne**    Mountains are his hobby. That and collecting maps.

**Luka** (*sarcastic*)    Collecting maps? Wow, how exciting.

**Suzanne**    Shhh. He can't help it.

**Ned** *and* **Theresa** *come over.*

**Theresa**    I could stay up here all day.

**Luka**    If there wasn't the football on telly at seven.

**Ned**    You had enough of the great outdoors?

**Luka**    It's not the same without my dog. (*He gets up.*)

**Theresa**    Ned and I have got something to tell you two. Haven't we?

*Pause.*

**Suzanne**    Have you?

**Theresa**    We've decided to go on holiday together . . .

**Suzanne**    That it? Thought you were gonna tell us you were getting married or something.

**Theresa**    Suzanne. That . . . that would be a bit hasty, wouldn't it . . . ?

**Suzanne**    Least I won't have to buy a bloody hat.

**Ned**    You'd have to be bridesmaid.

**Suzanne**    I would not!

**Ned**    Bridesmaid in DMs.

**Theresa**    We're talking about a holiday, that's all.

**Suzanne**    Where you going?

**Ned**    Snowdonia.

**Luka**    Been there.

**Suzanne**    Have you?

**Luka**    School field trip. For geography. It was all map reading and stuff.

**Suzanne** *gives* **Luka** *a nudge.*

**Theresa**    Was it nice? Snowdon.

**Luka**    S'alright. Mountains and that. Are we gonna go back to yours now then?

**Theresa**    You're in a bit of hurry, aren't you?

**Luka**    Too much fresh air always gets me depressed.

**Ned**    It's starting to get a bit nippy anyway.

**Theresa** *and* **Ned** *walk back towards where they've parked the car.* **Luka** *hesitates, kicking the football.* **Suzanne** *waits for him.*

**Suzanne**    Depressed?

**Luka**    Just thinking of my responsibilities.

**Suzanne**    The baby?

**Luka**    The baby, you and Scully.

**Suzanne**    Is Scully alright with kids?

**Luka**    Yeah . . . well, I guess so . . . I mean, she's never been around a baby . . .

**Suzanne**    So what – neither have I. There's a lot can go wrong with a baby. It's scary – the responsibility. I mean, you can't just like go out and forget to feed it.

**Luka**    You won't forget – it'll cry when it's hungry. Complete idiots manage to bring up babies, Suze.

**Suzanne** (*sarky*)    Well, thanks for the vote of confidence.

**Luka**    They're waiting for us. (*He starts to walk off.*)

**Suzanne**    Luka . . . if I was ill or something . . . you'd look after the baby?

**Luka**    Yeah, stop worrying, Suzanne. Come on.

**Luka** *exits. Still thoughtful,* **Suzanne** *follows.*


## Scene Two

**Theresa***'s kitchen. Morning.* **Theresa** *and* **Ned** *stand close together looking at a glossy coffee-table book with pictures of Mount Snowdon. An open map is beside them.*

**Ned**    Three thousand, five hundred and sixty feet above sea level.

**Theresa**    How high's Beachy Head?

**Ned**    Only five hundred or so feet.

**Theresa**    How come you remember stuff like that? You must have a head like an encyclopedia.

**Ned**    I've always been interested in general knowledge. And it's useful if we're stuck in traffic. You can tell the passengers some facts and figures about the scenery we're no longer passing. If you don't they all suddenly decide they need the loo. Old ladies are the worst.

**Theresa**    You don't have to be particularly fit to go on this kind of holiday?

**Ned**    No half the beauty of it is that you can take it at your own pace – enjoy the snowy peaks, the alpine flowers, the ravens circling above.

**Theresa**    It sounds lovely, Ned.

**Ned**    Now the first thing to do is get you kitted out with the proper pair of boots . . .

**Luka** *enters.*

**Theresa**    You're up early.

**Luka**    So are you two.

**Theresa**    When you get older it's harder to sleep. Too much going on in your head.

**Ned**    Yes there's no point in just lying around worrying . . . remembering what you used to have . . . (**Theresa** *looks at him.*) . . . just got to get on with it, haven't you? (*Pause.* **Ned** *checks his watch.*) Thanks for breakfast, Theresa.

**Theresa**    Not got to go already, have you?

**Ned**    Afraid I have. Unless I want a load of irate WI ladies gunning for me. Should be home around fourish though.

**Theresa**    Oh, oh right. Well, pop in then if you want, er . . . safe journey.

*He hesitates then goes and kisses her. They enjoy it, oblivious to* **Luka** *who is amused. As they part, he applauds.*

**Ned**    I'll be back for the encore later. See you, Theresa.

**Ned** *exits.*

**Luka**    Result. You finally got a shag!

**Theresa**    Shhhh.

**Luka**    Good was it?

**Theresa** *turns the pages of the book, pretending to be engrossed in the mountain pictures.*

**Luka**    Okay, okay, we won't go there. (*He puts some cornflakes in a dish. He sniffs the milk.*)

**Theresa**    Everything's fresh. You're not at Suzanne's.

**Luka**    Where you like unleash a plague every time you open the fridge.

**Theresa**    I keep saying I'll come up and stay for a couple of days but I don't know if I could stand it.

**Luka**    When I have kids I'll teach 'em to clean up after themselves.

**Theresa**    I did. Suzanne didn't used to be so chaotic you know . . . before she was ill . . .

**Luka**    Ill? Oh, her breakdown.

**Theresa**    She told you about what happened?

**Luka**    I've had a breakdown too. When I was twelve. I was back at my mum's and she had this really weird boyfriend. I got all paranoid about him. Thought he was gonna like try to kill me. I joined all these self-defence-type classes, bought big knives and stuff. Even started digging a pit in the garden to put him in.

**Theresa**    Oh my God . . .

**Luka**    So now he's under the patio, with geraniums sprouting from his brains.

**Theresa**    Don't talk daft.

**Luka**    No, I rang the socials and said get me out of here before I like kill the bloke. So they put me in a home – I'd been there about a week and I get stabbed by some headcase. Fourteen stitches and a ruptured spleen. You should've seen the huge great fucking hole and the yellow bits inside. Now that's my worst nightmare, having my guts cut out.

**Theresa**    You're putting me off my breakfast.

**Luka**    I couldn't be a woman . . . having a baby . . . in case I had to . . . you know, when they cut it out.

**Theresa**    A Caesarean. Two of mine came into the world that way. It's much the best way in my opinion.

**Luka**    Was your husband there? At the births.

**Theresa**    No. It wasn't so usual in those days.

**Luka**    I'd die. I couldn't watch. Disembowelment.

**Suzanne** *enters, huddled in her dressing gown. She looks rough.*

**Theresa**   You're up early.

**Luka**   Mr Bisset finally did the business, didn't he, Mrs Garner?

**Suzanne** (*flatly*)   Yeah? Congratulations, Mum.

**Theresa**   Coffee, love? With soya milk?

**Suzanne**   No. (*She sits down.*)

**Theresa**   You should have something . . .

**Suzanne**   You know I don't do breakfast.

**Theresa**   Every healthy living article you read . . . every one says the meal you should never miss is breakfast.

**Luka**   Miss breakfast – you die.

**Suzanne**   I'm just not hungry, okay? Jesus, why do you have to get at me all the time?

**Theresa**   Nobody's getting –

**Suzanne**   Just leave me alone.

**Theresa**   Suzanne . . . (*Pause.*) Suit yourself.

**Theresa** *exits.* **Luka** *puts his hand on* **Suzanne**'*s arm.*

**Suzanne**   Not got a fag, have you?

**Luka**   You can't smoke any more.

**Suzanne**   Shhh. (*She checks* **Theresa** *is out of the room.*) I feel a bit rough, y'know? Shaky.

**Luka**   You look it.

**Suzanne**   Look my age? Thanks. Didn't sleep at all last night.

**Luka**   Thinking of me?

**Suzanne**   Yeah.

**Luka**    So why didn't you come in? Your mum was round Mr Bisset's getting a shag. I heard her come in.

**Suzanne**    Don't. She woke me up at half past fucking two. It's gross thinking about it . . . She's my mother.

**Luka**    And you're my mother. And my baby's mother.

**Suzanne**    Don't, Luka.

**Luka**    Was that what was keeping you awake? Thinking about the baby.

**Suzanne**    No. No, I was thinking . . . but about other things . . .

**Luka**    Me too. 'Bout what Mr Bisset was saying to me last night . . .

**Suzanne**    Yeah, what were you two nattering about?

**Luka**    College. Business courses. NVQs. He said you can like phone up a lot of different colleges and they'll send you details. I was thinking about where I might go.

**Suzanne**    Right.

**Luka**    His son Michael did this business course and now he's got a top sales job. He's flying off to meetings in New York all the time.

**Suzanne**    Would you like that?

**Luka**    To go to New York? Flying business class.

**Suzanne**    Nice work if you can get it.

**Luka**    And I can, if I get the right qualifications. It's not like trying to get a job in a museum, Suze, that maybe employs five people. There's always work in business. Lots of well-paid work. I can see myself at college, I was just lying back and imagining it. (*A beat.*) So you were thinking of me, were you? Thinking horny thoughts . . .

**Suzanne**    Not really . . .

**Luka**    So, what were you thinking? Come on. Tell me.

**Suzanne**    I . . . I really do need to smoke. I'm going up the shop.

**Luka**    It's raining.

**Suzanne**    So. I'll get wet. (*She fetches her jacket.*)

**Theresa** *enters.*

**Theresa**    It's raining out.

**Luka**    She doesn't care.

**Theresa**    You can take my umbrella. It's by the door. Only don't lose it, it's a good one. Would you like to borrow a raincoat?

**Suzanne**    No, Mum, I wouldn't.

**Theresa**    But that jacket of yours isn't waterproof, and so thin. Couldn't get us a bag of jelly babies, could you, love?

**Suzanne**    What? Yeah, yeah.

**Luka**    And a Red Bull.

**Suzanne**    Mum? Can you . . .

**Theresa**    Lend you the money? There's nearly a quid's worth of change on the corner of the whatnot.

**Suzanne**    Okay. Ta. (*A beat.*) Bye.

**Suzanne** *exits.*

**Theresa**    I heard her being sick in the night.

**Luka**    What's new? I'll look after her, Mrs Garner.

**Theresa**    You'll make someone a good husband one day. Do you have a girlfriend yet?

**Luka**    Yeah.

**Theresa**    Is she nice?

**Luka**    Mrs Garner . . . could you lend us some money?

**Theresa**    Well, I . . . How much do you need, love?

**Luka**   I mean me and Suzanne. We want to get a caravan.

**Theresa**   A caravan? But she don't even have a car now . . .

**Luka**   A live-in caravan. Down here. Suze wants to move back down here to be near you.

**Theresa**   She's not said anything to me.

**Luka**   That's cos she doesn't want to worry you . . . You see it's our flat . . . there's been a lot of break-ins in the block. It's making her really like stressed and ill. She'd like to come back down here where it's safer. (*A beat.*) Could you lend her a couple of grand?

**Theresa**   Oh, I don't know. I have got a little bit put by like, but that's for when I get old . . . in case I have to go in somewhere.

**Luka**   You can come and live with us when you're old.

**Theresa**   And if I gave Suzanne money, I'd have to give the boys the same amount. To be fair, see?

**Luka**   She needs to move somewhere nice. It's so shitty where we live. It's not just the burglars. It's damp, it stinks, there's rats, the papers peeling, we've live fucking wires sticking out the walls . . .

**Theresa**   Can't the council –

**Luka**   They don't give a shit. If she lived somewhere nice, she'd eat properly. She wouldn't be so stressed out the whole time and I could get her to eat her breakfast. If it was quiet she wouldn't wake so early and she wouldn't be sick so much. We could go outside when we were getting on each other's tits, instead of screaming the place down. We could dance in the fields . . .

*The doorbell rings.*

**Theresa**   It'll be the milkman. He didn't call for his money last week.

**Luka**   You still have a milkman. Doesn't he get mugged?

**Theresa** *exits.* **Luka** *helps himself to more cornflakes, almost overflowing his dish. He mashes at them.* **Theresa** *enters carrying a bag of shopping.*

**Theresa**    The boy from the shop. Said we'd forgotten some more stuff. Said he must be mistaken, but he insisted. Must've been Suzanne.

**Luka**    Did he make you sign for it? He's such a wanker.

**Theresa** *(she clocks the cornflake mountain)*    You must be hungry. A growing lad, eh? How about a coffee – wash it down?

**Luka**    No thanks, Gran.

**Theresa**    'Gran' is it now?

**Luka**    Don't you like it?

**Theresa**    No . . . I mean, call me what you like . . . within limits of course. I'm just gonna see if I've still got that hat Suzanne left last time. She might be glad of it, weather stays like this.

**Luka**    When it stops, you could go to the building society, Gran. Get us the money.

**Theresa** *exits.* **Luka** *gets up. He opens the bag of groceries, takes out a box of chocolates. He is surprised. In the bottom of the bag is a coloured envelope addressed 'Suzanne'. He takes it out and opens it. It contains a card. He opens it and reads it.* **Luka** *pockets the card and puts the chocolates back in the bag. He puts his jacket on. He goes to the kitchen drawer, takes out a carving knife. He tries it out on a (wrapped) loaf of bread. Hearing* **Theresa** *approach, he hides the knife inside his jacket.*

**Theresa** *enters.*

**Luka**    If Mum comes back, I've just popped out a minute, okay?

**Theresa**    Do you want to borrow . . .

**Luka** *exits.*

**Theresa**    . . . an umbrella?

## Scene Three

**Josh***'s bedroom.* **Luka** *barges into the room, followed by* **Sophie**.

**Sophie**    Hey, you can't . . . ! (*Shouts out the door.*) Dad!

**Luka** *looks around the room.*

**Sophie**    I told you . . . he's not here. He should be at the shop.

**Luka**    He's not. I been there.

**Sophie**    Why did you hit him?

**Luka**    He pissed me off. Looking down his fucking nose at me. (*He laughs.*)

**Sophie**    What do you want with him? (*Pause.*) I'm getting Dad to throw you out. I can't believe he let you in. Stupid pissed bastard.

**Luka** (*takes out the little car and reads*)    'Suzanne, I must see you again. I'll be at the shop all Saturday morning –'

**Sophie**    See?

**Luka**    '– or you could drop by my house later maybe. In case you can't remember the address, it's . . .' What a fucking wanker. (*Pause. He puts the card away.*) Did you know?

**Sophie**    My brother and your mum? I was so shocked.

*He swings round to face her.*

And you know what? I think he's in love with her.

*He sits down on the bed.*

What're you gonna do?

**Luka**    Wait.

**Sophie** (*leans on the wall*)    Well, you can't wait here. (*Pause.*) Why do you have such a problem with it anyway? (*Pause.*) I think it's sweet. (*Pause. There is a crash, off. She looks out the door.*) Dad's fallen over. (*She comes in and sits down on the edge of* *the bed. He doesn't look up.*) You're crying. Are you? (*She moves closer to* **Luka**.) Hey . . . (*Pause.*) Do you wanna talk about it?

*He reaches and feels the beads of the bracelet on her wrist. He looks up at her, discovering her watching him intently.*

**Luka**   You've got your brother's fucking nose.

**Sophie**   No.

**Luka**   And in a couple of years you'll be like your old man – too fat to get up the stairs.

**Sophie**   Fuck off. I'm really fit.

**Luka**   A fit girl.

**Sophie**   I work out. After school. See. (*She flexes her (small) muscles.*) And. . . (*She pulls up her top, flexes her stomach.*)

**Luka**   Who do you think you are – Jennifer Lopez? Wait till you have a Caesarean.

**Sophie** (*pulls her top down*)   A what?

**Luka**   Show me your tummy again.

**Sophie**   No.

**Luka**   You're shy.

**Sophie**   Me? (*She shakes her hair back, sits back, he puts his hand under her shirt, strokes her tummy with a finger.*)

**Luka**   Your tummy's really soft.

**Sophie**   You've cold fingers.

*He breathes on his fingers, she giggles. He brushes her cheek with them.*

**Luka**   Warmer?

**Sophie**   Warmer.

*He strokes her face, then kisses her. She responds eagerly. They kiss hungrily. He starts to undo her trousers.*

**Sophie**   Don't.

**Luka**   What? I'm not doing anything. (*He strokes her face.*) Trust me.

**Sophie**   This is Josh's bed . . .

**Luka**   Did he bring her here?

**Sophie**   Your mum? No, no . . . (*She turns **Luka**'s face back to her.*) I don't think so.

**Luka** *lifts **Sophie**'s T-shirt again, kisses and rubs his cheek against her tummy.*

**Sophie**   Dad'll go ballistic.

**Luka**   He'll never get his fat arse up the stairs.

*She giggles, strokes his hair. He lies her back on **Josh**'s bed and climbs on top of her.*

**Sophie**   We can't . . . no, I mean . . . we can't!

**Luka**   Can't we?

**Sophie**   No . . . we shouldn't . . .

**Luka**   It's meant to be.

**Sophie**   I'll get pregnant . . . hey!

**Luka**   Yeah, I'll use a condom, okay.

**Sophie**   You've gotta . . .

**Luka**   It'll be good, it'll be fine. . .

**Sophie**   You will? You better . . .

*They continue kissing and caressing.*

**Luka**   That's great . . . really great . . . oh hang on . . .

*Astride **Sophie**, **Luka** unzips his jacket and pulls out the carving knife. **Sophie** looks up and sees. She screams.*

**Sophie**   Fuck! Oh my God, no . . .

**Luka** (*chucks the knife on the floor*)   Don't want to go disembowelling myself, do I?

**Sophie**   Jesus. I don't believe . . .

**Luka**   S'alright, I'm not Jack the Ripper. I brought it to cut your brother's dick off.

**Sophie**   Dad'll have heard me . . .

**Luka**   He won't. It's okay. (*He kisses her.*)

**Sophie**   If he comes up here I'll die.

**Luka**   Relax. There . . . You're beautiful, you're really very beautiful.

**Sophie** *puts up her arms to embrace him. They start making out, rather uncomfortably.*

**Sophie**   Luka . . . it's . . . ow . . .

**Luka**   It's okay, baby . . . it's fine . . .


## Scene Four

*The shop. The sign on the door is turned to 'closed'.* **Suzanne** *paces outside the shop with her umbrella up.* **Josh** *enters with the keys.*

**Suzanne**   You're supposed to be open. Where've you been?

**Josh** (*flatly*)   Walking.

**Josh** *opens the door, holds it for her. He watches her pass him and go to the shelves. He turns the shop sign to 'open'.*

**Suzanne**   Gotta get one or two things. Provisions.

**Josh** *goes behind his counter.* **Suzanne** *takes a basket and starts shopping.* **Josh** *watches.*

**Josh**   So? How's it going?

*Struggling with her resolve,* **Suzanne**'s *thoughts aren't on shopping. She takes a loaf of bread, then another, then discards them.*

**Josh**   Everything okay?

**Suzanne** *puts a pack of sandwiches in her basket, then another, then another.*

**Josh**   Having a picnic are you? All those sandwiches.

*Moving out of* **Josh***'s sight,* **Suzanne** *starts filling her basket, just picking up anything and stuffing it in.*

**Josh**   It's a bit rainy for picnicking today. Might clear up later, I suppose. (*Pause.*) Okay, you don't want to talk. Okay. But if you can't pretend I don't exist, you can't pretend we never happened . . .

**Suzanne** *emerges from behind the shelves with an overflowing basket of shopping. She staggers to the counter with it and plonks it down.*

**Josh**   You want all of this?

**Suzanne** *takes another basket and goes back to the shelves.* **Josh** *hesitates, then follows her.*

**Josh**   Suzanne.

**Suzanne** *starts pulling things from the shelves, causing a massive box-and-can avalanche.* **Josh** *rushes over to her.*

**Josh**   What are you doing?

**Suzanne** *gathers up a handful of groceries defensively.*

**Josh**   You don't need all this. Three Fairy Liquids? (*He tries to take them, she holds on. He gives up.*) What's the matter?

**Suzanne** *drops the bottles in the overflowing basket she has discarded on the floor.*

**Suzanne**   Nothing is the matter. (*She picks up some more bottles of washing-up liquid.*)

**Josh**   And I suppose I'm gonna have to put all this back. (*Pause.*) Are you angry with me? Was it my note? (*He walks away from her.*) I don't know what it is you want.

**Suzanne** *drops the bottles into the basket.*

**Josh**   What is it, Suzanne? Is it me you want? (*Pause.*) What do you want?

**Suzanne** *takes a packet of biscuits from the shelf.* **Josh** *grabs hold of it, they struggle over it, he pulls it away from her.*

**Josh**   Do you want Hob Nobs? (*He thrusts them back at her, takes another packet of biscuits from the shelf.*) Or Rich Tea Fingers?

*She reaches for it. He continues to thrust packets of biscuits at her, pulling them away and trying to take those she's already clutching.*

**Josh**   No, no you can't have them both. Or would you rather have Malted Milks? Large or small packet? Chocolate-covered or plain? Decision time, Suzanne. How about digestives? Digestive creams?

*She grabs hold of him, shakes him.*

**Suzanne**   I don't know what I want! You bastard, don't do this to me! I want to be happy. What's wrong with that? (*She releases him.*) I'm on the fucking slide.

**Josh**   And you what? You want me to catch you? I'll catch you, I'll stop you . . .

**Suzanne**   I'm thirty-five years old and I'm sliding.

**Josh**   Okay, I thought you'd come here because you wanted me. (*He walks away from her.*) You better go. Leave all that. I'll put it back later.

**Suzanne** *crouches down, looking at the basket. Pause.*

**Josh**   Suzanne . . . ? Suze?

*She ignores him. Reluctantly he returns to her. She looks up. She's crying.*

(*Shaky.*)   Help me. I'm not going back. I'm no good for him . . . (*She looks at* **Josh**.) I'm no good for anybody . . .

**Josh**   No . . . no . . . (*Awkwardly he cuddles her.*) It's okay . . .

**Suzanne**   I need to be strong. Help me be strong.

**Josh**   You are strong, Suze . . .

**Suzanne**   If I stay, there's the baby Luka . . . he'll end up just like me – he won't get to college, or if he does, the noise, the baby – he won't be able to do his homework, he'll have to get a job to buy all the things the baby needs, he'll have to drop out. You don't get many chances . . . and I'm taking his chance away. Josh, don't let me go back. (*She gets up.*) Will you come to the station with me? Will you see me off?

**Josh**   Where are you going? Back home . . . ?

**Suzanne**   No. No, I know some people in . . . No, I'm not gonna say. In case he finds out. I mustn't see him again. I . . .

*She sobs,* **Josh** *comforts her.* **Luka** *enters with Sophie.*

**Luka**   Mum.

*She starts, pulls away from* **Josh**. **Luka** *catches hold of* **Sophie** *and snogs her. He stops and looks at* **Suzanne**. *For a moment she just stares, then slowly she gets up and walks towards him.*

**Luka**   You slag.

*She slaps him.*

**Suzanne**   I . . . I'm . . . giving up everything for you. You bastard. Bastard!

**Luka**   Giving up everything? What exactly have you got? Or do you mean shop boy here? You've had him, haven't you, bitch?

**Josh**   Don't call her/ a bitch!

**Suzanne** (*indicating* **Sophie**)   /How old is she? (*She looks towards* **Sophie**, *then grabs* **Luka** *by the hair.*) She's just a kid, you stupid bastard.

**Luka** *pushes* **Suzanne** *away from him, just holding his temper.*

**Luka**   Don't you. Don't, Suzanne.

**Suzanne**   I love you.

**Josh**   Oh/ shit.

**Sophie**   /Gross.

**Luka**   Fuck you! Fuck you, bitch!

**Sophie** (*goes over to* **Josh**)    My God, Josh . . .

**Suzanne**    Look at me, you little shit. You're all I think about. Living with you and dancing in the fields.

**Sophie**    Jesus.

**Luka**    Did you fuck him?

**Josh** *is about to say something.*

**Sophie**    Leave it, Josh.

**Suzanne**    Are you listening to me?

**Luka**    Did you –

**Suzanne**    Did you fuck her? You little cunt. (*A beat.*) It was never gonna work, Luka. Was it? Tell me it was never gonna work. Give me that at least.

**Josh** *returns to his counter.*

**Suzanne**    Admit that somewhere inside you knew it . . . knew that we've both been so . . . battered, so disappointed . . . and fucking shat on that it was never gonna work, no matter how hard we tried . . .

**Luka**    You tried? When did you try, Suzanne? It's like 'Hallo, did I miss something?' When did you try to make things better? When did you try to get us some money?

**Suzanne**    It's not about fucking money!

**Luka**    You're a loser.

**Suzanne**    And what exactly are you?

**Luka**    I'm a cunt, I admit it.

**Suzanne**    We're both cunts. And we're having a baby. We can't even be good to each other. What would it feel like having us as parents? Would you want to be our kid? (*She walks away from him.*) Would you? I know I sure as hell wouldn't. It's gonna be hell for that baby. (*A beat.*) It's not right. I shouldn't have it. I'm not having it.

**Luka**    You are.

**Suzanne**   It probably hates me already. It's probably listening right now.

**Sophie**   Shit . . . /you're having his baby.

**Luka**   /Stop it, Suzanne. You're having it.

**Suzanne**   No, I can't, not now –

**Luka**   I'm not letting you get rid of our baby.

**Suzanne**   'Our baby' – our baby while you're out there shagging someone else's little girl? (*She starts to leave.*) Christ Luka, you make me sick.

**Luka**   Where are you going? (*He blocks her way.*) You're not killing my baby.

*She tries to move past him. He pulls out his knife.*

**Sophie**   No, Luka!

**Josh** *moves in front of* **Sophie** *protectively.* **Suzanne** *laughs.*

**Suzanne**   Whoa, that makes sense. You'll kill me and save the baby. (*She rolls up her shirt, exposing her belly.*) That's where it is, right there. Our little boy or girl. Why don't you cut it out and rescue it from me. You want the baby? You want the fucking baby . . . come and get it . . . come on.

**Josh**   Suzanne, for fuck's sake . . .

**Suzanne** *advances on* **Luka**, *takes the knife blade in her hand, tilts it to her belly.*

**Suzanne**   You want to hurt me, fucking do it. You want to be the one that breaks this thing – do it, Luka.

**Sophie** (*to* **Josh**)   Press the alarm!

**Suzanne**   Gonna spill my guts? Come on.

**Sophie**   Josh!

**Luka** *is shaking. He can't look at the knife, nudging* **Suzanne**'s *belly. She snatches it from him by the blade, cutting her hand. She wipes the blood on* **Luka**'s *face. He is frozen in shock. Pause.*

**Suzanne**    A vow in blood. It's the end. I swear. (*Looking at* **Luka**'*s horrified, frightened face, she drops the knife.*) Oh. Oh God. (*She wipes* **Luka**'*s face.*) I'm sorry, baby. (*She kisses her hand and plants it on her belly.*) And I'm sorry, little baby.

**Josh** *edges forward and picks up the knife. He takes it back to the counter, takes a cloth and goes back to* **Suzanne**.

**Josh**    Look – your hand. (*He wraps the cloth around her hand.*) You should sit down.

**Sophie** *brings a chair over.*

**Suzanne**    Luka . . . (*She reaches out to him. He doesn't look at her. She sits.*) . . . It's gonna be okay.

**Josh**    That's right.

**Suzanne**    I know what to do.

*Pause.*

**Josh**    We could have a beer.

**Sophie** *gives the other three a beer each. They open them and drink, in their own space and time, silent, introspective, no one wanting to break the truce.* **Suzanne** *looks at her belly, puts her hands on it.* **Luka** *snatches a glance at her while she isn't looking.*

*The shelves slide back to reveals* **Ned** *and* **Theresa**. **Ned** *is in his coach driver's uniform. He brings* **Theresa** *a cup of tea.*

**Ned**    Have I put too much milk in?

**Theresa**    No, that's lovely. It's a lot of money . . . and it was what I'd been saving up . . . It doesn't feel right . . . to give it all to her . . .

**Ned**    Both your boys are doing well, aren't they?

**Theresa**    Yes. Oh yes.

**Ned**    Well I don't suppose a couple of thousand would make such a difference to them . . .

**Theresa**    No, but there's being fair, especially when there's my grandchildren to think of. I don't know what her father would've said . . . well I do. I really don't see it working Ned.

**Ned**    Oh I do. I don't think Suzanne's doing so badly. In fact I admire her.

**Theresa** *is about to sip her tea, but stops, surprised.*

**Ned**    She looks after that boy, that can't be easy. And the previous ones . . that very quiet girl who used to eat her hair . . .

**Theresa**    Zoe. Poor little thing.

**Ned**    Kids like that would've probably been in care if they weren't staying with Suzanne.

*Back in the shop.*

**Suzanne** *walks to the counter.*

**Suzanne**    I won't hurt the baby . . . I couldn't. I'll look after your baby, darling. I promise.

*She opens the till.* **Sophie** *looks at* **Josh**.

I'll do the best I . . . I'll do better.

**Suzanne** *takes out a big wad of notes.*

**Suzanne**    You're right. Money matters.

*Back to* **Ned** *and* **Theresa**.

**Ned**    You should be proud of her.

**Theresa**    Yes . . . I suppose I am . . . in some ways. She's just different.

*Back to* **Suzanne**.

**Suzanne**    I'll find a caravan by the sea.

*The stage transforms into* **Suzanne**'s *caravan.* **Suzanne** *and* **Luka** *are dancing to the Red Hot Chilli Peppers. The others join them.*

*Music cuts out and everyone leaves. Sound of the wind over the cliffs.*

**Suzanne** *is left alone facing the future.*

# PLAYWRITING MATERIALS

This material is for people who want to write. Over the years, Out of Joint and the Royal Court have collaborated with many play-wrights, both established and unknown. We asked some of them what advice they might give to other writers. The result is this collection of exercises, tips and stories:

**Judy Upton**
Start writing plays

**Simon Stephens**
Discover your character

**Rebecca Prichard**
What is their story?

**April De Angelis**
'Hot-seat' a character

**Stephen Jeffreys**

**Mark Ravenhill**
Delay the conflict

**Simon Bennett**
Toilet paper and a pen

**Max Stafford-Clark**

**Caryl Churchill**

# JUDY UPTON
## START WRITING PLAYS

This is a newcomer's guide to playwriting. If you would like to write a play, but you don't know where to start, here are a few things I've learnt. If you know most of this stuff already, or if you have no intention of writing a play, just skip it. Okay?

The only way to get started in playwriting is to write a play - as opposed to just thinking about writing one some day.

I started writing dialogue as a child, making plays to record on cassette tape, usually a story about robbers or a haunted house. The sound effects were the biggest attraction - though beware that the flushing of a toilet can make a brilliant torrential rainstorm until it starts going 'glug glug' and upstages everyone. Robbers and haunted houses were not a big feature in my young life, but most plays we read at school were about kings, wars or life in an exotic land, not about ordinary people from Ordinaryville. Soon I realised that there were things I wanted to say about my own world - dramas happening to me and to people around me. You don't have to stick to what you know, but that was what fired me up. As a child I hadn't been to the theatre (apart from the panto), and as far as I knew no one from my school ever became a writer. It certainly wasn't presented as a career option.

Maybe it is a good idea to keep secret your early efforts at playwriting. That way there is no pressure. No one can ask if you've finished it or whether they can read it. You can take your bunch of characters and get them talking to each other. But what about? Some writers know in advance and have everything plotted out. Others start at the beginning and just see what happens. There are no rules, but there are books to give you advice about structuring a script and other practical tips. I found them useful.

Try to see plays, especially new plays. This is not easy if you live out in the wilds, but it is essential at least now and again. If you can't see many plays because of the travelling and expense, read them in the library.

When your script is ready to show someone, the Writers' Handbook and Writers' and Artists' Yearbook (in most libraries and bookshops) list many theatre companies that are willing to read new plays. Send it out. You have nothing to lose.

Fringe theatre companies are more likely to produce a first play, but the companies can be harder to locate. Listings in London's Time Out and internet search engines tend to come up with possibilities. It helps to hang out in pub theatres (if there are any near you).

It is worth contacting your local arts board to find out about local playwriting groups. Writers' groups can be great - or not. A great group might offer readings, workshops and visits from guest speakers. The bad group has a know-all who tells you how to completely rewrite your script. Also, meetings are spent discussing what it's like to be a writer. But it's better to be at home writing than discussing being at home writing.

If you write to literary agents, they may tell you they are currently unable to take on new clients. But this changes miraculously once you land a professional production or if you win a big prize. An agent will usually take you on when the first contract arrives, and I would advise you to get an agent then. Why? Is this an honest business to work in, or is it a pool of sharks? You've guessed it.

On the subject of prizes, my advice is to enter every competition going. There are a fair number listed in the Writers' Handbook and on the Writernet website. The odds are not too bad, and better than a 'write-a-caption-and-win-a-fridge' competition.

Well, that's about it. Except to add that if you want to be a playwright - persevere. Make sure someone is always looking at a piece of your writing, and keep going. Don't keep rejection letters, they'll only become a fire risk. If you receive criticism and you are unsure whether it is constructive, then look for a second and a third opinion. If you decide that playwriting is not for you, fair enough. But if you don't try, you'll never know.

Judy Upton's plays include Ashes and Sand (1994), Bruises (1995) and Sliding with Suzanne (2001), all published by Methuen.

*

*Go for it! There is nothing to lose. Find out, using the internet or a library, where to send a script (agents and theatres). Just go for it. You may be rejected, but all they can say is 'No' and if not - 'Yes!'*
ROSA RANKIN-GEE, AGED 14, ROYAL COURT YOUNG WRITERS' PROGRAMME.

# SIMON STEPHENS
DISCOVER YOUR CHARACTER

It strikes me that the only qualification you need to start as a playwright is to be fascinated by people. For many writers this fascination becomes an insistent and maddening obsession. You don't get paid shit to write plays. You have to be driven by more than a desire to make money. And if you are driven, then what may drive you most fruitfully is a compulsion to stare at other people and wonder how the hell they ended up like they did.

Spend a minute thinking about the character you are writing. When your minute is up, write down 51 things that you know about your character. Don't let your pen leave the paper. Don't let yourself stop.

You will start writing obvious things. The first twenty or so may simply record facts or features of your character that you already know. Then (around number 25) things start to get interesting. You will find it becomes harder. You will want to stop. Don't. Just force yourself to write something. You may find that the facts and features between about 25 and 45 start to become remarkable, fascinating, oblique, silly, odd or curious, but also (somehow) true.

You may not use these facts and features directly in the script. But discovering your character will inform every word you write. The details may not make it into your final draft, but don't panic. You may not taste the gas in a bowl of soup heated over a gas hob, but cold soup tastes terrible - just like a play with thin and undeveloped characters.

Simon Stephens' plays include Bring Me Sunshine (1997), Bluebird (1998), and Herons (2001) which is published by Methuen.

\*

*Write about stuff that you'd like to see that isn't happening. Rather than think 'Well, obviously no one wants that sort of theatre'. If it's not being done, why isn't it being done?*
POLLY WISEMAN, ROYAL COURT YOUNG WRITERS' PROGRAMME.

## REBECCA PRICHARD
WHAT IS THEIR STORY?

I learnt this exercise from Fiona Macbeth - and I like it because it's so simple and because it encourages people to trust their ideas and instincts (hopefully) and to think about relationships, drama, what's alive in the relationship between audience and characters... and all that good stuff.

What is their story? Ask participants to move their chairs to the back of the room and form an 'audience'. Ask two volunteers to stand 'on stage' in front of the audience.

Volunteer 'A' stands upstage looking at a fixed point behind or above the audience.

Volunteer 'B' stands a few steps behind 'A' looking at their back. They freeze in this position. Ask the audience 'what is their story?' Tell them to say the first thing that comes into their head and encourage them with further questions; What is the relationship between A & B? Where are they? Are they strangers or do they know each other? What do you think is about to happen? What has just happened? Challenge the audience to take their stories as far as they can, building on each other's ideas or contradicting one another.

Tell 'B' to take a step or two towards 'A' (perhaps putting a hand on their shoulder, keeping change to a minimum). 'A' then makes a minimal movement (such as turning their head or repositioning their eyes). 'A' and 'B' freeze in this position.

Ask the audience: has their story changed?

Follow this with a discussion. How often do we project stories onto people we know nothing about? How do we read body language? Did you enjoy guessing - as an audience? Were you active? Why did the story change? How much does an actor have to move to change a story? Is there a heightened relationship between an actor and an audience? Can you play with this as a playwright? Is your audience a 'character' to think about when writing plays?

Rebecca Prichard's plays include Essex Girls (1994), Fair Game (1997) and Yard Gal (1998), all published by Faber.

## APRIL DE ANGELIS
'HOT-SEAT' A CHARACTER

For this exercise, each participant starts by creating a character. Ask them to explore some questions when creating a character, such as:
- Are they male or female?
- Are they a child, young, middle-aged or old?
- Where do they live? (Country, city, house, flat, homeless?)
- Do they work? What work do they do? (List jobs.)
- Can you picture them now? What are they wearing? Picture them from head to foot.
- Are they happy, sad, angry, bored, mad, confused, overjoyed?
- What are their likes and dislikes?
- Where did they grow up? What was their childhood like?
- Do they have a life surrounded by people? Do they have friends?
- Are they alone a lot? Are they lonely?
- Do they have secrets or problems? Name them.

Then add some more questions.

Let the group 'hot-seat' one or two volunteers. 'Hot-seating' is a process where you ask them questions that they must answer in character. If they do not know the answer yet, they can say so.

First, the group 'hot-seat' each other in pairs. Then each participant identifies for themselves their character's greatest hope and fear. After this, they must imagine a scene where their character meets another character who could somehow bring about this greatest hope or fear.

A volunteer can help improvise the scene. Alternatively, each participant can write the scene. One way to test a newly written scene is to ensure something has changed between the beginning and the end of the scene.

April De Angelis' plays include Hush (1992), The Positive Hour (1997) and Playhouse Creatures (1997), which are published by Faber in the collection De Angelis: Plays One.

## STEPHEN JEFFREYS

1) Begin by thinking of a place. It could be indoors or outdoors; a place you know well or a place you have seen in a photograph or in your imagination. Try to avoid obvious locations like kitchens and living rooms.

Now imagine that place as it might be represented on a stage. Perhaps some details are omitted, perhaps the representation is very simple. In your mind, move from your original picture to your stage picture and back again.

Think about the atmosphere of the place. Does it feel different early in the morning or late at night? How is the place affected by different weather conditions?

2) Take a pack of playing cards and remove all the Aces and Court cards (King, Queen, Jack). Pick two cards at random. These represent the two characters who will be in the scene:
- a low card indicates a shy, introverted person.
- a high card indicates an outgoing, extrovert person.
- a heart indicates someone who lives through their emotions.
- a diamond indicates someone who lives through their brains.
- a spade indicates someone who lives physically (the five senses).
- a club represents someone who lives through their intuition (the sixth sense).

So, a four of hearts could be an emotional character who is quite withdrawn. A nine of spades would be a confident, physical type.

Think about who these people might be: decide on their names, age, sex and occupation. Add some details from your imagination and observation.

3) Now imagine one of these people in your space - maybe the one who seems more at home there. Think what they might be doing in the space. Try to give them a physical activity - perhaps a piece of work, or a repeated neurotic action, or a relationship with an object that is part of your place.

Now imagine the second character coming in. Imagine the entrance carefully . Is the first person surprised by the entrance? Or has a meeting been arranged?

Now ask yourself what might happen between these two people. Try to create a situation which forces them to meet again, or where a task is set or an offer made. This will be the centre of the scene.

Now think which person might leave first. Or do they both stay or both leave together? This is the end of the scene.

4) Think of the shape of the scene in three parts:
    i) The meeting
    ii) The centre
    iii) The end

How much time does each take? There are many possibilities. They could spend most of the time on preliminaries, and only reach the centre of the scene after trying to avoid it. Or they could get to the point very early and then have difficulty leaving each other. Choose the shape that seems most appropriate.

5) Now, very quickly, write down two accounts of what happens in the scene, one for each person. Write down the physical actions each performs and the thoughts and feelings they have. These accounts may be very different. At the end, decide what each person really wants from the encounter. Does what they want change as the scene goes on? Re-write your account of the scene if you change your mind about a character's intention.

6) Now write the dialogue, bearing in mind exactly what each character wants at each point. Think of them as having actions when they speak, i.e. flattering, confronting, evading, befriending, amusing, teaching. Try to give each character a distinctive rhythm and vocabulary.

Read your scene and rewrite it if necessary. Don't be afraid of cutting out dialogue which seems interesting but which doesn't help the scene.

7) When you've finished, think what happens before and after this scene. Maybe this scene is the beginning of the play - maybe it's the whole play.

This is one way of writing a scene or a play. It begins with the idea of the theatre as a physical space and uses chance (the cards) to help stimulate your imagination. Equally you could begin with a theme, a character you know, or a line of dialogue.

Stephen Jeffreys' plays include Valued Friends (1989), The Libertine (1994) and I Just Stopped By to See the Man (2000), all published by Nick Hern Books.

# MARK RAVENHILL
## DELAY THE CONFLICT

I was about fifteen when I first thought about writing a play. I was about thirty when I first got round to finishing one. Even allowing for a bit of laziness, this is a long time. Of course, I started plays regularly, but after a few pages they would sort of fizzle out and I couldn't work out why.

I reckon this was mostly because I'd read in a book somewhere or been told by a teacher that 'drama is conflict'. So I would set out to write scenes of conflict. What this really meant was the play never had anywhere to go because the characters just blocked each other - they shouted until they were hoarse, and then the play was over after just a few pages.

But then I realised 'drama is delayed conflict'. On the whole, human beings want to lead comfortable lives. We avoid uncomfortable truths, we want things to carry on much as they are. It is only when really pushed that we confront things, and even then we try to duck out of doing anything about it. Finally, when we have run out of options, we commit ourselves to conflict (and the world may be better for it). For example, in Shakespeare's Hamlet it is only at the end that Hamlet is ready to fight, and in Caryl Churchill's Top Girls it is only at the end that Marlene is ready to have the big argument with her sister.

This pattern of avoiding the truth, being confronted by the truth, delaying the conflict and finally committing to the conflict - this is not the only pattern for writing a play. But it is a lot more useful than 'drama is conflict'.

Mark Ravenhill's plays include Shopping and Fucking (1996), Handbag (1998) and Some Explicit Polaroids (1999), all published by Methuen.

\*

*Write a short scene where something happens. For example, a girl tells her dad that she is pregnant. But you have to write the scene three times: first, where she tells him at the beginning; second, where she tells him in the middle; and third, where she tells him at the end. See how different it is where you place the action. That's the exercise that helps me the most.*

JACK HEALY, ROYAL COURT YOUNG WRITERS' PROGRAMME.

## SIMON BENNETT
TOILET PAPER AND A PEN

Where did I get started? A prison cell is as good a place as any, I suppose. A sheet of toilet paper and a ballpoint pen. Throw in a bit of boredom and you've got yourself a potential writer.

I had in the past, long before my prison sentence, written stuff down and always felt that one day I'd write a novel. At this point in my life I had never read a play, only novels and short stories. The sort of life I was living didn't allow much space for writing. Then came prison where I was physically confined within its walls and rules. You are told when to wake up, when to have your daily meals, shower and gym. Everything is laid on. The only thing you have to aim for is your release date. But within the walls and rules is a freedom. No rent or bills to worry about, nothing to do but explore your mind, to piece together all the bits of your life you find so confusing on the outside. Most importantly, to discover the talent we are all supposed to have: a talent that outside life buries beneath the restricting confines of the rat race.

So there you have it, if you want to be a writer - get nicked a few times, do a bit of bird, then write about it. A bit of life experience never hurt anybody.

How did I start? Well, I started by rewriting a Tracy Chapman song on a piece of toilet paper, more out of boredom than any artistic urge. My first discovery was that I quite enjoyed it, and soon after I was writing my own poetry. Once in prison I joined an English class. I was encouraged by a teacher who seemed to like my poems. She even asked if she could take them home and show her husband. I remember her saying that I should not let it go once I got out.

By the time of my release I had written a few short stories, including one about a burglar, which was probably the origin of my play Drummers. The date was 3 August 1989. I wondered what I would be doing in ten years' time.

Once out, I started an 'A' level theatre studies class at Merton College and (would you believe) I fucking passed it, which was amazing as I was semi-illiterate at the time. During this course I read my first play (John Osborne's The Entertainer) and I thought rather cheekily that I could do better, and wrote the first draft of Drummers.

From there I went to the Royal Court Young People's Theatre where I acted in a play called Wildfire. It was developed through improvisation by the actors and put on the page by the writer Jonathan Harvey and director Ian Rickson. It was a valuable experience. This led to me join the Royal Court Young People's Theatre and its writers' group in the evenings. I was given the opportunity to hear my words out loud and get immediate feedback, which is essential in developing a writer and their craft.

Putting Drummers on the back burner for a while, I wrote another play called Tattooed Tears and entered it in a competition at the Bush Theatre, and I was one of the finalists. This was very encouraging, but most importantly I made a contact, and that contact was Joanne Reardon, then literary manager at the Bush. Joanne suggested I should get an agent and recommended a few names. One was Rachel Daniels at London Management. I sent her my latest draft of Drummers with a letter explaining a bit about myself. Suddenly I had an agent.

Rachel sent Drummers to Out of Joint and a geezah called Max something or other. With his help I developed Drummers further. After a few meetings, Max cracked open the wine and declared that he was going to put on the play. At last I could truly call myself a writer, and got myself just as truly pissed that evening.

Ten years after my release, on 4 August 1999, I am sitting in the dark of the Arts Theatre, Cambridge. The music starts and the actors take the stage. The lights go up, the music stops and my words fill the theatre. Prison happened to another person in another life, a long, long time ago.

Simon Bennett's Drummers (1999) is published by Nick Hern Books.

*

*Observe life. Always carry a notebook, and if you hear a piece of dialogue - something someone might say on the bus - write it down. Go to art galleries. Pick up on visual images and gradually you will create a visual bank. Use everything around you.*

LEO BUTLER IS A MEMBER OF THE ROYAL COURT YOUNG WRITERS' PROGRAMME. HIS PLAYS INCLUDE MADE OF STONE (2000) AND REDUNDANT (2001).

## MAX STAFFORD-CLARK

I'm often asked what happens when a writer and director disagree in rehearsal, as if this is unprecedented and would result in the collapse of a production. It is true that disagreements occur in rehearsal, as they do in a marriage. But not every disagreement leads to a divorce. I was trained in the Royal Court tradition, where the director's primary job is to realise the intentions of the play-wright. The director's ideas must spring from discussions between writer and director.

The director is a new figure in the theatre, and the job has evolved differently in different countries. In Russia, the director is the senior figure whose concept is the starting point for a production of a classic or a new play. In Germany, the dramaturg works with the writer on the play before it goes into production, cutting and re-editing the script. In England, it is the director of a new play who is responsible for the relationship with the writer. For an emerging writer sending a script to a theatre, the first contact is often the literary manager who responds to the script by letter or at a meeting. The theatre may offer a rehearsed reading which gives the writer a chance to hear their work for the first time and offer an opportunity for actors to engage with the play.

For the director, the process of working on a new script varies from play to play. Some plays, such as Caryl Churchill's Blue Heart (1997) or Sebastian Barry's The Steward of Christendom (1995), hardly changed from delivery of the script to the first performance. Other plays have different requirements. For example, at the first rehearsal of Mark Ravenhill's Some Explicit Polaroids (1999), the actors read two scripts: some characters appeared in one version, others in both. Once Mark had eliminated one of these story lines, the task in rehearsal was for each actor to follow through the writer's outline and even suggest the middle and end of their character's journey. Mark Ravenhill was responsive to the actors' early work and made use of rehearsals to explore different situations.

Some writers like to test their work before going into rehearsal. Both Mark Ravenhill and Patrick Marber (Dealer's Choice, 1995) have used extensive workshops before rehearsals start. During this time they may cut and edit the play, discard a story line or use actors to research a character in greater depth.

It is the director's responsibility to make collaboration possible and enjoyable. A director must also share and guide contributions from the set designer, the lighting designer and the sound designer to give focus and weight to the production. Collaboration does not happen naturally, and it has to be encouraged and led. It is hard work. This is why some directors only choose to direct classic plays where there is no danger of disagreement with the writer. It is also part of the reason why some writers direct their own plays.

There are many different ways of working on the production of a new play but, at its best, theatre is a team game, not an individual sport. It is cricket rather than tennis.

Max Stafford-Clark is the director of Judy Upton's Sliding with Suzanne and artistic director of Out of Joint.

\*

## CARYL CHURCHILL

When I was eight there was a piece in the paper about a girl of thirteen who'd had a book published - I thought thirteen was extremely old. I was already writing stories and poems and went on writing and at the same time liked going to see plays. It was when I was a student that I started writing plays rather than anything else and my first four plays were done by students. I read a lot of plays and went to rehearsals of all kinds of productions. After university I wrote some plays that weren't done and some that were done on the radio. If a play wasn't accepted at once, I didn't rewrite it but just forgot about it and wrote another one. I didn't have a lot of time to write as I had small children, and most of what I wrote was short. My 'first' professional stage play, Owners at the Royal Court, was something like my fifteenth or twentieth play and I was thirty-four.

Caryl Churchill's plays include Top Girls (1982), Serious Money (1987), This is a Chair (1997), Blue Heart (1997) and Far Away (2000). Her plays are published either by Nick Hern Books or by Methuen in two collections, Churchill: Plays One and Churchill: Plays Two.

## ROYAL COURT YOUNG WRITERS' PROGRAMME

Established to ensure that the theatre maintains its position as a magnet for originality, vitality and flair, the Royal Court Young Writers' Programme (YWP), as the youth, community and education department of the Royal Court, has been part of the driving force behind the theatre's mission to embrace and produce new writing from all sections of society.

Based at THE SITE, a studio space next to the Royal Court Theatre in Sloane Square, London SW1, the YWP runs playwriting groups for 13 -16 year olds and 17- 25 year olds. Under the guidance of professional playwrights and directors, young people explore their individual voices and styles, writing about what is important to them. There are opportunities for plays to be given public readings and productions performed by professional actors. No previous experience is necessary.

Scripts can be submitted to the YWP by anyone under the age of 26, at any time of the year.

The YWP also co-ordinates and implements a full programme of education activities and events, such as matinees, discussions, work-shops, resource packs and INSET training.

For further information on the YWP and/or the education programme:

Write to The Site, Sloane Square, London, SW1W 8AS
call 020 7565 5050
email ywp@royalcourttheatre.com
or visit the Royal Court Website at www.royalcourttheatre.com